The Bridge Between Worlds

A Journey Beyond Time; Healing the Past to Free the Present

Fiction or Real?

You Decide:

The Origin of

The Loveday Method®

The Thirteenth Book

The Origin of The Loveday Method

The Library, The Crystal and The Coat of a Thousand Lives; Threads of the Forgotten

Author: Geoffrey Loveday

Copyright © 2025 by Geoffrey Loveday - All Rights Reserved.

The right of Geoffrey Loveday to be identified as author of this work has been asserted by the author in accordance with section 77 and 78 of the Copyright, Designs and Patents Act 1988.

First Published in 2025
ISBN 978-1-917978-15-6 (Paperback)
978-1-917978-16-3 (Hardback)
978-1-917978-17-0 (E-Book)

Book cover designed and layout by: Geoffrey Loveday

Published by:

Mindlayers Publishing
35-37 Ludgate Hill,
London, England,
EC4M 7JN

Website: www.liverpoolhypnosis.co.uk

Authors and publishers cannot be held responsible for any consequences that result from the usage of information in this book.

The author or the publisher assumes no responsibility or liability for how you use the information contained herein.

A CIP catalogue record for this title is available from the British Library.

All rights reserved. No part of this book may be reproduced or translated by any form or by any means, electronic or mechanical, including photocopying, recording or by any information storage and retrieval system without written permission from the author.

The novel is entirely a work of fiction. The names, characters, and incidents portrayed in it are the work of the author's imagination. Any resemblance to actual persons, living or dead, events or localities is entirely incidental. The views expressed by the fictional characters do not necessarily reflect the views of the author.

I wonder where life will take us now ...

And so the journey begins.

Let me take you on this magical adventure.

Contents

About the Author 10

Dedication 12

Inspiration 16

Why I Had to Write This 19

Part 1 19

    Chapter 1: Author's Invitation 19

        Preface – The Beginning of the Loveday Method 21

    Chapter 2: The Revelation 26

    Chapter 3: A Question That Changes Everything 29

    Chapter 4: The Loveday Method 31

    Chapter 5: The Origin of the Loveday Method 33

    Chapter 6: The Coat of Hidden Weight 39

    Chapter 7: Are You Carrying the Echoes? 41

Part 2 44

    A Grandmother's Song 44

    An Uncle's Mischief 47

    An Aunt's Embrace 49

    A Father Never Known 52

    The Thread That Connects Them All 55

Part 3 56

    Chapter 8: If You Wonder Why I Wrote These Stories ... 56

    Chapter 9: How It Works 58

    Opening the Doorway 58

    Stepping Into the Story 60

    Releasing and Returning 62

Now You Begin to Understand 63

Chapter 10: Into the Magic of Life 66

Chapter 11: A Journey Through Time 67

   Ann's Hidden Burden.. 69

Part 4: 72

   Chapter 12: Ann's Journey.. 72

      Releasing and Returning 84

      The Light of Peace.. 89

   Chapter 13: Preparing for the Second Journey – Beyond the Veil.. 99

      The Island of Light.. 102

      Into the Deep Trance 103

      Ann's Journey – In Her Own Words...................... 104

      Ann's Journey – The Island of Red Light.............. 112

      Ann's Journey – The Valley of Orange Light 116

      Ann's Journey – The Valley of Yellow Light 118

      Ann's Journey – The Valley of Green Light 119

      Ann's Journey – The Valley of Blue Light.............. 121

      Ann's Journey – The Indigo Light 123

      Ann's Journey – The Violet Crown......................... 125

      Ann's Journey – Entering the Rainbow................. 128

      Ann's Journey – The Gift in the Rainbow 130

      Ann's Journey – Returning to the World............... 134

   Chapter 14: The Third Session – The Akashic Library 136

      Ann's Journey – The Akashic Library 138

Ann's Journey – The Chair and the Drop Through Time 141

Ann's Journey – The Weight of Injustice 144

Ann's Journey – The Threads of Time...................... 147

Ann's Journey – Wrapped in the Rainbow 150

Ann's Journey – Returning Home 152

Chapter 15: The Fourth Session – The Enchanted Spectacles... 154

Ann's Journey – The Enchanted Spectacles.............. 156

Ann's Journey – Through the Enchanted Spectacles 159

Ann's Journey – The Release................................... 161

Ann's Journey – Cutting the Thread........................ 164

Ann's Journey – The Rainbow of Renewal 166

Ann's Journey – The Gift of Forgiveness.................. 168

Ann's Journey – The Return of Forgiveness 171

The Guide's Reflection 172

Chapter 16: – The Book of Echoes................................. 173

Ann's Voice – The Book of Echoes 174

Ann's Journey – The Echo of a Forgotten Ancestor .. 176

Part 5... 179

Chapter 17: An Invitation to You, the Reader............. 179

The Bridge of Time... 183

Part 6... 185

Chapter 18: The Journey Beyond Time 185

Where the Loveday Method Has Taken Me 186

Part 7... 192

Chapter 19: Ann's Journey – The World Beyond Time ... 192
- The Guide's Reflection ... 199
- The Truth Behind the Journeys ... 200
- The Bridge Forward ... 202

Part 8 ... 204
- Chapter 20: Epilogue – The Awakening ... 204
  - Author's Note – A Message from the Heart ... 208
  - Dedication ... 211
- Chapter 21: A Sign from the Universe ... 212
  - Reflection – What the Dolls Taught Me ... 217
  - The Threads Continue ... 218

Part 9 ... 221
- Chapter 22: The Bridge Between Worlds – A New Beginning ... 221
  - Final Words – Until the World Listens ... 224
  - The Dawn of Remembering ... 226
  - *Closing Quote* ... 228
  - About the Author ... 229

About the Author

My name's Geoffrey Loveday. Like you, I'm on a journey – one shaped by life's beauty, its ache, and the quiet search for meaning that runs through it all.

This is my thirteenth book. Seriously, I've lost count. I've earned professional titles, gathered credentials, and spent years in this work. But none of that really explains *why* I do it. The truth is, there's a small, steady voice inside me – ancient and alive – that keeps asking me to write. Not to impress, but to connect. To tell the truth. To offer something real.

I don't write because I have all the answers. I write because I believe that truth – honest, raw, human truth – is sacred. I believe healing begins with honesty. And I believe that when we share our stories from the heart, we remember we're not alone.

My work isn't about fixing anyone. It's about helping people find their way back to what's already inside them – the parts untouched by noise, pain, or expectation.

Underneath all of it, there's a deep wholeness. There's stillness. There's *you*.

Through The Loveday Method and Inherited Therapy, I don't come as a guru or a healer. I come as someone who's been there – someone still learning, still beginning again. As a certified hypnoanalyst, clinical hypnotherapy instructor, and witness to thousands of personal transformations, I've seen what's possible when we stop forcing change and start remembering who we are.

Lasting change doesn't come from striving – it comes from remembering. From returning. From reconnecting with the truth we've carried all along.

I don't see myself as special. But I do know this calling is real. And I share what I've learned with the hope that it finds the people who need it most.

This is my work. This is my offering. And I'm grateful you're here.

Dedication

This book is a tribute – an offering – to the extraordinary souls who have shaped my life with quiet strength, deep wisdom, and boundless love. You live not only in my memories, but in my breath, my choices, and my voice. You live here, in these pages.

To my father – your calm, steady presence lives on within me. Though your voice has fallen silent, I still hear it in moments of stillness; I still feel your hand guiding mine. You taught me the power of quiet love – the kind that doesn't need to be loud to last. The kind that anchors, steadies, and stays, long after the words are gone.

To my mother – our time together was brief, but your light burned bright and true. You taught me to hold beauty gently, to recognize what matters, and to let tenderness lead. Your grace still moves through my life like a soft current – subtle, constant, and alive.

To my grandparents, aunts, and uncles – your stories, your love, your laughter became the ground beneath my feet. You gave me roots, belonging, and the deep knowing of where I come from. That sense of home travels with me everywhere.

To Alma and Leon – your open hearts welcomed me without question. Your quiet generosity and steady warmth left marks on my life that no words can fully express. Thank you for showing me how love expands to include, to heal, to hold.

To my beloved wife – though you now walk beyond this world, you remain ever near. I feel you in our children's laughter, in the hush before morning, in the strength I didn't know I had. Your faith in me is still my compass, guiding me through every new beginning. You are in every word, every breath, and every line of this book.

To our children – you are my why. My strength. My greatest teachers. You've shown me that love is not fragile – it bends, stretches, and grows, even through the pain. In you, I see hope embodied, and I am endlessly grateful.

To my grandchildren – your wonder brings light into every shadow. Your joy reminds me that life renews itself, that love carries forward, and that the future is still unfolding in beauty.

To my sons-in-law – thank you for choosing to stand with us, not just in name, but in heart. Your presence enriches our family in quiet, meaningful ways that never go unnoticed.

To my brothers – I carry your absence with reverence. The ache of missing you is matched only by the strength your memory gives me. Your laughter still echoes in me. Your pride still steadies me. You are with me in every step forward.

To my friends, mentors, and fellow travelers – your belief in me has been a lifeline. Through both the quiet and the storm, your presence mattered. Thank you for holding space – for reminding me of who I am when I momentarily forgot.

This book belongs to all of you as much as it does to me.

Your love is its rhythm. Your influence, its spine. Every word carries the quiet gratitude of a life shaped by you.

Thank you – for your love, your light, and your legacy.

Inspiration

This book was born from quiet heroism – the kind that lives in hospital corridors and waiting rooms, in bedside whispers, and in long nights filled with uncertainty. It is a tribute to those walking through illness with courage, grace, and a strength that words can never quite contain.

If you are fighting, recovering, or simply finding your way – you are the heart of these pages.

To those who have shared your journeys so openly – you've given more than your stories. You've given us a window into the resilience of the human spirit. You've shown that bravery doesn't always roar; sometimes it moves in trembling hands, soft footsteps, and the quiet decision to try again, even when the way forward is unclear.

To the doctors, nurses, researchers, and medical professionals – your dedication goes far beyond medicine. You don't just treat illness – you restore dignity, nurture hope, and often give people back their lives. Your work ripples outward, touching hearts, changing futures, and reminding us what compassion in action truly looks like.

To the carers, families, and loved ones who keep showing up – you are the unseen strength behind every recovery, the quiet force that steadies others when they falter. Your patience, loyalty, and countless acts of love define what real courage looks like.

To the organisations and charities that advocate, educate, and support – you are the lifeline many never expect but come to depend on. Your compassion creates lasting change – the kind that can't be measured in numbers, only in lives touched and hearts lifted.

To my readers – thank you for opening this book with curiosity and care. By reading these stories, you become part of something larger – a movement toward empathy, understanding, and healing. Your willingness to listen creates space for others to be seen.

And to those behind the scenes – mentors, editors, loved ones – thank you. Your belief turned an idea into something real, something that might reach the people who need it most. Your trust and support have meant more than words can express.

This is more than a book. It is a celebration of the human spirit – of the will to keep going, to keep loving, to keep hoping, even when the path ahead is uncertain.

Thank you – for your courage, your compassion, and your presence in this shared story of being alive.

Why I Had to Write This

Part 1

Chapter 1: Author's Invitation

Before you begin, take a breath. Let the noise of the world fall away for a moment. What you hold in your hands is not simply a book – it is a doorway.

Every story within these pages was born from a place beyond ordinary memory. They came through dreams, through whispers, through moments when the veil between worlds grew thin. Many have called them fiction, and perhaps that is what they seem. But if you listen closely, something inside you may recognise them – not as fantasy, but as remembrance.

For these are not just stories. They are echoes. Echoes of the lives we have lived before, and of the lives still waiting within us to be remembered. Each echo carries love, loss, courage, and the hope that healing is possible.

The *Loveday Method* grew from these echoes – a way of travelling beyond the surface of the mind, into the deeper currents of the soul. Through it, people have stepped through doors they did not know existed. They have met ancestors they thought long gone, released grief they did not know they carried, and found light where they once felt darkness.

What you are about to read will ask something of you – not belief, but openness. You do not have to accept every word as truth; you only have to feel. Because when the heart listens, the soul remembers.

As you journey through these pages, imagine that each word is a key, each story a path, each breath a step closer to the forgotten parts of yourself. Perhaps you will find answers here. Perhaps you will find questions. Or perhaps – as many before you have discovered – you will find *yourself*.

The bridge between past and present is already beneath your feet. The light of the future is waiting at the far end.

All you need to do is begin.

Preface – The Beginning of the Loveday Method

People often ask me how all of this began – when I first realised that we can travel through time not with machines or science, but through memory, emotion, and spirit.

The truth is, I never set out to create anything. I was simply searching for understanding – for a way to make sense of the pain I saw in others, and the pain I felt within myself.

For years I worked with people who carried sorrow they could not name. They would say, "I don't know why I feel this way – it doesn't belong to anything in my life." Their words stayed with me. How could someone feel grief, fear, or guilt that didn't seem to have a source?

One night, while sitting quietly in meditation, something extraordinary happened. I felt a presence – not outside me, but around and within me – as though the air itself had shifted. Images began to rise, not as memories, but as scenes from another life. I saw faces I didn't know but somehow recognised. I felt their joy, their pain, their love. It was so real that when I opened my eyes, I could still smell the air of that other time.

That moment changed everything.

I began to explore gently, working with people in deep relaxation, inviting them to trust what surfaced from within. Slowly, patterns appeared. They were not random visions, not dreams or fantasies – but living connections, threads woven across generations.

A woman who had always feared water discovered the memory of an ancestor lost at sea. A man who carried endless guilt saw himself as a soldier, torn by choices made long before he was born. When they spoke their truth, when they forgave and released, something remarkable happened: their symptoms eased, their hearts opened, and their lives changed.

It was as though by healing the past, they were freeing the present.

That is how the Loveday Method was born – not from theory, but from experience. It is not hypnosis, not therapy, not religion. It is a conversation between the soul and time itself. It asks only one thing of you: to listen with an open heart.

Over the years, I have been humbled by what I've witnessed. People reunited with loved ones long gone. Ancestors finding peace after centuries of silence. Grief transformed into gratitude, fear into light.

I do not claim to understand every mystery this work reveals. All I know is that it changes lives – and it changed mine.

If you are reading this, it may be because a part of you is already ready to remember. Perhaps the stories that follow will stir something in you – a knowing, a recognition, a quiet whisper that says, *yes, this is true.*

You do not need to believe in anything to begin. Just allow. Just listen.

And so, the journey begins – not backward or forward, but inward, into the timeless space where love never dies, and every soul is waiting to be remembered.

Over the years I have been blessed to share many books with the world. *The Book of Echoes. The Coat of a Thousand Lives. The Enchanted Spectacles. The Book of the Unknown.* Each one poured out of me as if the stories had been waiting, pressing against the veil, asking to be told.

When people read them, their responses were strikingly similar. They would write to me, or stop me in person, with eyes wide and hearts unsettled, and say:

"This can't just be a story. It feels too real."

Time and again, I heard it. Some readers said they wept for reasons they couldn't explain. Others spoke of memories surfacing, of people they had lost suddenly standing beside them as the words unfolded on the page. A few even admitted they had to close the book at times because the presence they felt was so powerful, so immediate, it frightened them.

And yet, alongside the fear, there was always a pull. A recognition. A whisper of truth.

You see, these books were never intended as fantasy. They are not inventions of my imagination. They are transmissions – doorways disguised as novels. Within their pages are the voices of ancestors, the weight of forgotten coats worn by countless lives, the laughter of loved ones we thought gone but who remain close, just beyond our sight.

The stories are alive.

Every chapter carries echoes of real lives lived, of emotions still vibrating in the unseen world. Every scene is a thread connecting you to something – or someone – greater than yourself.

Readers sensed this long before I dared to say it aloud. They knew, in their bones, that they weren't simply being entertained. They were being remembered. They were being called.

And now, at last, I can speak the truth plainly: **my books are not fiction. They are invitations.**

Invitations to step across the threshold of story into lived experience. To journey back through time. To feel what your ancestors felt. To discover the roots of your suffering. To reconnect with the love that has never left you.

This is the purpose of my work. This is the promise of every page you hold.

Chapter 2: The Revelation

For so long, I allowed others to call my books "fantasy." It was easier that way. Safer. People are comfortable with fiction; it lets them keep one foot in the ordinary world while peeking into the extraordinary.

But the truth will not stay hidden forever.

The stories I have written are not fantasy. They are not inventions. They are **real**.

Every book – The *Book of Echoes, The Coat of a Thousand Lives, The Enchanted Spectacles, The Book of the Unknown,* and many others – is more than words on a page. They are **portals**, doorways cut into the fabric of time, carrying truths that stretch far beyond my own life.

When you open these books, you are not only reading. You are entering. You are stepping across a threshold into spaces where memory and spirit are alive, where the past breathes again, where the unseen waits patiently to be recognised.

Within their pages are echoes of real lives, fragments of ancestors who once walked this earth and who still walk beside us. The feelings you experience as you read – the sudden wave of grief, the flash of joy, the strange familiarity of a character you have never "met" – these are not accidents. They are transmissions. They are messages, carried on the current of the story, reaching from one soul to another.

The veil between worlds is thinner than you think. Stories slip through it like light through a crack. They bind us to what came before and what lies beyond. They remind us that we are not separate, not alone, not bound only to the present moment.

And so I say it plainly now: **my books are real, and they are waiting to be lived.**

If you feel their pull, it is because a part of you already knows the truth. The stories are not outside you. They are *within you*. They are part of your bloodline, your spirit line, your deepest remembering. They call you because they belong to you.

Through them, you will discover what has always been there: the love of those who came before, the unfinished stories still seeking completion, and the healing that awaits when you choose to walk back through the doorway.

These books are not entertainment. They cannot escape. They are returning.

And if you are willing to step through, they will carry you to places you thought were lost, to voices you thought were silenced, to truths you thought were forgotten.

The stories are alive. The portals are open. The journey begins the moment you say yes.

Chapter 3: A Question That Changes Everything

Pause for a moment. Place your hand on your heart. Feel the weight you carry there – the grief, the fears, the anxieties, the longings you cannot name.

Now let me ask you:

What if those feelings are not yours alone?

What if the sadness that floods you at night is not born from your life, but from the life of someone who came before you?
What if the fear you cannot shake was once the fear of an ancestor, pressed into your blood like a hidden signature?
What if the longing that aches inside you is the echo of a dream left unfinished, a story left untold generations ago?

We are taught to believe our suffering belongs only to us. That our pain begins and ends within the span of our own years. But what if that is not true? What if you are carrying the unwept tears of your grandmother, the unsung prayers of your grandfather, and the unshed laughter of a forgotten child whose story was never finished?

What if your life is not just your own, but a tapestry woven from countless threads of those who lived, loved, struggled, and hoped before you?

If that is true – and I tell you, it is – then the weight you feel can also be lifted. Because what has been carried down through generations can also be released. And what has been hidden in silence can finally find its voice.

This is why the stories I write are more than stories. They are maps. They are doorways. They are **invitations** to walk back into the lives of those who came before you, to feel what they felt, to understand what they endured, and to set free what has been holding you bound.

So I ask again:

What if the feelings you carry are not yours alone? And what if, by stepping into these stories, you could finally return them to the place they belong?

Chapter 4: The Loveday Method

For as long as I can remember, the stories pressed against me, whispering to be told. They came as visions, dreams, and sudden waves of emotion that felt too vast to belong to me alone. At first, I believed they were fragments of imagination. But the more I listened, the more I recognised them as something greater: voices carried across time, reaching through me to be heard.

For years I poured them into books – The *Book of Echoes, The Coat of a Thousand Lives, The Enchanted Spectacles,* and others. Readers told me they felt transported, as if they had stepped into another dimension. Many admitted they had wept, or trembled, or felt the presence of loved ones leaning close as they turned the page.

Still, the question lingered: *Why were these experiences happening? And how could I help others enter them more fully, not only through story but through direct encounter?*

The Loveday Method is not a technique of the mind. It is not about closing your eyes and imagining, nor about pretending or playing with fantasy. It is something far older, far truer.

It is a **sacred pathway** – a doorway that opens when you are ready to step beyond the narrow lens of ordinary perception and enter the vast, living current of memory that flows through your blood and spirit.

This is not invention. It is recognition.

Through The Loveday Method, you are gently guided into the spaces where your ancestors still breathe. You will find yourself standing inside the emotions they once carried – the love they poured into their families, the grief they buried in silence, the wisdom they held close to their hearts.

And as you walk their paths, you begin to see how their stories are still woven into your own. The fears you carry, the longings you feel, even the unspoken grief you cannot explain – all of these may be threads passed down through time. The Loveday Method reveals these hidden threads and allows you to hold them in the light.

It is more than healing. It is remembering.

Remembering who you are at the deepest level. Remembering where you come from – not just in name or lineage, but in soul and spirit.

Remembering that you are never alone, for you are surrounded by a river of love that has flowed through generations, a love that cannot die, a love that has never left you.

This is the heart of The Loveday Method: not fantasy, not illusion, but a living return. A return to truth, to love, to the timeless bond between you and those who came before.

Chapter 5: The Origin of the Loveday Method

The Loveday Method was not something I set out to create. It was something that revealed itself to me when I least expected it – in a moment when my own life was weighed down by grief I could not explain.

For years, I carried a sadness that did not belong to any single event in my own story. It was like a shadow in my chest, rising in quiet moments, flooding me without warning. I searched for reasons – perhaps it was my own losses, perhaps old wounds I thought I had forgotten. But no matter how I searched, I could never find the root.

Then, one night, something shifted.

I was sitting in stillness, surrounded by silence so heavy it seemed alive. A memory rose before me – not of my own life, but of a man's. His hands were rough with work, his face weathered by hardship. I felt his exhaustion, his despair, as if it were my own. And then I realised: it was not a memory *of mine* at all. It was the memory of one who had come before me.

He was my ancestor.

I felt his grief pour into me like water through an open door. His sorrow became my sorrow, his pain my pain. But in that same moment, I also felt something else – a bond so deep it dissolved the distance between us. I was not imagining him. I was *with* him. I could feel his breath, his heartbeat, his tears.

And then, something extraordinary happened.

I spoke to him. I told him he was seen. I told him his suffering had not been in vain. I thanked him for surviving long enough to pass life forward to me. And as I spoke, the grief began to lift – not only from him, but from me. It was as if the two of us were healing together, across the great river of time.

When the vision faded, I was left trembling, but lighter. The shadow in my chest was gone. What remained was a warmth, a presence, a knowing: *I am not alone. I have never been alone.*

That night was the seed of what I now call **The Loveday Method**.

From that point on, I began to listen differently. When emotions rose that did not belong to me, I opened to them, asking, *Whose story is this? Who wants to be heard?* Slowly, a process began to take shape – a way of entering the river of ancestral memory with intention, of walking alongside those who came before, and of bringing back not only their stories but their love.

It was never about invention. It was never about pretending. It was about listening – and remembering.

And that is how The Loveday Method was born: not from theory, but from lived experience. From the day I discovered that the veil between myself and my ancestors was thin, and that by stepping through, we could both find healing.

We often think of inheritance only in material terms – the colour of our eyes, the shape of our hands, the family heirlooms passed down through generations. But there is another kind of inheritance, quieter, unseen, yet far more powerful.

We inherit suffering.

Grief, trauma, fear, shame – these are not emotions that vanish when a life ends. They have weight. They leave marks.

And when they cannot be expressed, when they cannot find a voice, they slip silently into the fabric of the family line, carried forward like invisible threads woven into the next generation.

Think of the grandmother who lost a child but was never allowed to mourn. She dried her tears in silence, hiding her grief because the world demanded her strength.

That unwept sorrow does not simply disappear. It lingers. It waits. And years later, her grandchild feels waves of sadness with no name, no reason, as if crying someone else's tears.

Think of the grandfather who endured war, who carried horrors he could never speak aloud. His body returned, but a part of his spirit remained on the battlefield.

Unable to unburden himself, he held it in his blood, his breath, his bones. And in time, his descendants carried that same unease – the restless vigilance, the unshakable fear – without ever knowing why.

Think of the mother who longed for freedom, who had dreams she was never allowed to pursue. She buried her desires beneath duty. And generations later, her children find themselves restless, aching with a longing they cannot explain, living under the weight of unfinished dreams.

These are not isolated stories. They are the hidden stories that live inside all of us.

Science now tells us what the spirit has always known: trauma can be encoded in the body, written into the very DNA we pass on.

But long before science gave it a name, we felt it. We lived it. We carried the weight of voices that were silenced, wounds that were never healed, tears that were never cried.

This is why you sometimes feel emotions that do not belong to you. This is why you carry burdens that make no sense in the context of your own life.

They are not illusions. They are inheritances. They are echoes of lives once lived, waiting for release.

And here lies the gift: if suffering can be inherited, so too can healing. By turning toward these echoes with love, by stepping into their stories and giving voice to what was once silenced, we can free not only ourselves, but all those who came before and all those yet to come.

The pain is not only yours. The healing does not need to be only yours, either.

Chapter 6: The Coat of Hidden Weight

Imagine a coat.

Not an ordinary coat, but one stitched from the fabric of generations. Every ancestor who came before you has added something to it. A patch of grief sewn here. A lining of fear stitched there. A button of longing, a sleeve of silence, a collar of unspoken dreams.

This coat has been passed down through time. Worn by those who lived before you, worn by those who survived what could not be named. And when they could no longer carry it, they handed it to the next in line.

Now it rests on your shoulders.

At first, you may not even notice its weight. You think it is simply part of who you are – the heaviness in your chest, the ache in your bones, the sadness that arrives without warning. But over time, the coat begins to press down. Its fabric thickens with the uncried tears of your grandmother, the unspoken fears of your grandfather, the unheard prayers of forgotten kin.

You did not choose this coat, yet you wear it. And because it has always been there, you may mistake it for your own skin.

But here is the truth: **the coat is not who you are.**

It is an inheritance, yes – but not a destiny.

Through The Loveday Method, you are invited to look at this coat clearly for the first time. To trace its threads, to feel the hands that stitched it, to honor the stories woven into every seam. And then, with love, to loosen the fabric. To set down what is not yours to carry. To fold the coat with gratitude and return it to the ancestors who gave it to you – not in rejection, but in release.

And when the coat is lifted from your shoulders, what remains is not emptiness but lightness. Freedom. Breath. The space to clothe yourself in your own truth, your own life, your own love.

The past may have given you the coat. But you are the one who decides whether to keep wearing it.

Chapter 7: Are You Carrying the Echoes?

Pause for a moment and look within.

Have you ever felt a sadness that seemed to rise from nowhere – a heaviness in your heart with no clear cause?

Have you ever carried fears that did not make sense in the context of your own life – anxieties that seemed older than you, deeper than your own story?

Have you ever longed for something you could not name – a dream you never lived but still yearn for, as if it belonged to someone else?

These are the echoes.

They move quietly through you, surfacing in your thoughts, your emotions, even your body. They show up in the patterns you cannot explain – the relationships that replay the same struggles, the obstacles that appear again and again, the shadows you cannot escape.

Perhaps you cry at songs whose words mean nothing to you, yet stir tears as if they were written from your soul.

Perhaps you walk into a place for the first time and feel a shiver of recognition, as though your feet have already walked those stones.

Perhaps you have known grief for someone you never met, or love for a face you have only seen in an old photograph.

These are not accidents. They are not illusions. They are not "just in your head."

They are the unspoken emotions of those who came before you, carried forward in silence until they find voice in you.

They are the griefs that were never grieved, the traumas that were never healed, the loves that were never expressed.

You are the vessel in which they rise again, asking not to burden you, but to be acknowledged at last.

If you recognise this within yourself, know this: you are not broken. You are not imagining things. You are carrying the echoes – and within those echoes lies the possibility of release.

The Loveday Method is the key. It allows you to step into those echoes with clarity and compassion, to meet the ancestors whose stories you are carrying, and to return the weight that was never yours to hold.

So I ask you now: **Can you see the echoes within you? And are you ready to transform them into freedom?**

Part 2

The Loveday Method has led to countless encounters with those we believed were lost to us. Each story is unique, yet all carry the same truth: when the veil lifts, love comes rushing through.

A Grandmother's Song

One woman I guided came to me carrying a sorrow so old, so heavy, she could not name its source. It was like a shadow stitched into her chest, a grief that had no story, no beginning, no end.

As the journey unfolded, she sat quietly, her breath shallow, her heart trembling. Then, somewhere in the stillness, she heard it: a melody – so faint it could have been mistaken for wind slipping through an open window.

But it was not the wind.

The notes gathered, weaving themselves into a tune she had not heard in decades. It was the lullaby her grandmother used to hum when she was a child – a song that once carried her into sleep, safe in arms that felt like home.

The sound wrapped itself around her, soft and insistent, until it was no longer only music but presence. She felt arms enfold her, exactly as they once had.

She smelled lavender, her grandmother's favorite scent – sweet, calming, impossible to mistake.

Her body shook as the tears came. Not tears of sadness alone, but tears of recognition. She whispered through her sobs, *"She's here. She's holding me."*

This was not memory. Memory lives in the mind, faint and fragile. This was something else entirely. This was a reunion. A love stepping across the veil, alive, undeniable.

In that moment, the sorrow she carried found its origin – and its release. For what she thought was absence was in truth a presence waiting patiently, humming the same song until she was ready to hear it again.

An Uncle's Mischief

There was a man who came to the Loveday journey carrying a heaviness he could not shake. Life had shaped him into someone serious, burdened, always responsible. His family admired him for his strength, but he admitted to me he had not laughed – truly laughed – in years.

As the session unfolded, silence wrapped around him. Then, suddenly, the quiet was broken by a sound – a ripple of laughter, rich and booming, bursting into the room as though the walls themselves were shaking with joy. He startled, eyes wide. It was a sound he knew, though he had not heard it since childhood.

It was his uncle's laugh.

The uncle who had been the family's trickster, the teller of wild jokes, the one who made the children squeal with delight and the adults roll their eyes while secretly smiling. The uncle who had died young, leaving behind a silence that weighed on everyone.

The man doubled over, unable to hold it back. He laughed until his body shook, until tears streamed down his face. Between gasps he said, *"That's him. He's teasing me again. He's here."*

What returned to him that day was not only his uncle's presence, but a part of himself that had been locked away – the part that knew how to laugh without reason, to be light in a world that can be heavy. His uncle had come back to remind him: joy is an inheritance, too.

An Aunt's Embrace

Another woman entered her journey carrying a loneliness that seemed bottomless. She spoke of being surrounded by people, yet still feeling unseen, untouched, adrift – as though a vital thread of her life had been cut. No friend, no partner, no family member could reach that hollow place inside her.

As she sank deeper into the process, her body stiffened. Her breath caught. For a moment, she trembled, unsure whether to resist or surrender. Then, almost imperceptibly, her face softened. Her lips parted, and she whispered with awe, *"There's fabric... brushing against my cheek."*

Moments later her voice cracked, thick with emotion: *"Arms. Arms around me."*

Her tears came suddenly, uncontainable. It was her aunt – the one who had loved her with a mother's tenderness, the one whose passing had left a wound no one else could soothe. In that instant, she felt the unmistakable warmth of her aunt's embrace. It was not the vague recollection of a hug. It was the weight of real arms, the press of real fabric, the heat of living presence.

Then came the fragrance – delicate, unmistakable. The faint sweetness of rosewater, her aunt's perfume. The scent filled the space, surrounding her, enveloping her in a cocoon of familiarity and love.

And finally, the words. Not imagined, but arriving with the clarity of truth she had longed for her entire life:

"I am still with you. I never left."

Her sobs deepened, but their quality shifted. They were no longer the tears of loneliness. They were the tears of release – the kind that cleanse, that soften, that heal. The cavern of emptiness she had carried for so long was no longer empty. It was full – full of presence, full of love, full of the knowing that what she feared lost had never truly gone.

When she emerged from the journey, her entire being felt lighter. The hollow place in her heart was no longer a wound but a doorway – a space where love flowed freely, endlessly, without end. She carried with her a truth she would never again forget: **love is never severed. It may be hidden, but it waits patiently to be remembered.**

A Father Never Known

My own journey brought me into the presence of an ancestor I had never known in life – a man whose name was spoken only in whispers, tucked away in the corners of family stories. He was more absent than presence, more silent than memory. And yet, in the unfolding of The Loveday Method, he came.

At first, he appeared only as a shadow, indistinct and formless, standing just beyond my sight. He watched quietly from a distance, and though I could not yet see him, I could feel him – like a current in the air, a weight in the silence. Slowly, step by step, he drew nearer. The shadow thickened, sharpened, until the outline of a man began to take shape.

His features revealed themselves in fragments: a strong jaw softened by kindness, eyes steady with both sternness and compassion, a presence that was both commanding and deeply tender. There was no need for introduction. I knew. He belonged to me, and I belonged to him.

I did not fully understand what I was seeing – but I understood what I was feeling. It was as though a great hand pressed firmly against my back, steadying me, rooting me. A warmth spread through my chest – not fleeting, not fragile, but strong, grounding, like sunlight breaking through storm clouds after years of rain.

At that moment, something inside me shifted.

This man was not only my ancestor. He was my guide. My protector. The father I had longed for but never thought I would find. His presence carried pride, unmistakable and fierce, as though he had been waiting across generations for me to finally turn and see him.

And then I heard him – not with ears, but with the language that lives deeper than words, the silent voice that speaks directly to the heart:

"You are not walking alone. You never have. I am here."

The words rippled through me, undoing years of silent ache. The wound of fatherlessness I had carried – the emptiness I had tried to fill in a thousand ways – loosened and fell away like a garment I no longer needed. I was no longer searching, because I had been found.

In that moment I realised: the love I thought I had missed had always been here. It had flowed quietly through the bloodline, through memory, through the unseen spaces of my life, waiting for the moment I was ready to feel it.

And when I did, I understood – death had not erased him. Time had not stolen him. His presence was alive, patient, and eternal.

The Thread That Connects Them All

Each of these stories is different – a song, a laugh, an embrace, a steadying hand. Yet they all reveal the same truth: presence is real. Love endures. Those we thought gone are never truly lost to us.

Through the Loveday Method, these reunions are not fantasy but lived experience. They remind us that while grief may tell us we are alone, the deeper truth is this: **we are always held, always connected, always loved.**

Part 3

Chapter 8: If You Wonder Why I Wrote These Stories

If you are wondering why I wrote these stories – why I kept returning to that insistent river of voices, images, and scenes – here is the simple truth: I wrote them because they would not leave me in peace.

You may ask: *Can one truly communicate with the dead?* I am here to say **yes.**

Not in the way that sensational tales or parlour tricks might suggest, but as something far gentler, far more profound: a quiet, living conversation that crosses the veil between one world and the next.

The journeys I describe in these pages are not fanciful inventions. They are not exercises in memory. They are real.

When I first began writing, I thought I was inventing stories. Yet the words arrived with a weight that did not belong to imagination. They carried the scent of a room, the cadence of a voice, the details of lives I had never known yet felt in the marrow of my bones.

The line between past and present blurred. Grief and joy surged through me as though they were mine, though I knew they belonged to others.

I discovered there is a language older than words: a language of presence. It speaks in the warmth of a breath against your cheek, the brush of a hand upon your shoulder, the silence that says more clearly than speech: *I am here.* Those who have gone do not vanish; they remain close, woven into the fabric of our days.

Through the Loveday journeys, I have walked with them, listened to them, and brought their stories back into the light.

So if, while reading, you feel your chest tighten, or your eyes fill with tears, or your heart leap with sudden recognition of a face you never knew – do not dismiss it.

Lean towards it. These are not tricks of memory. They are encounters. They are reunions.

This is why I wrote these books: to offer a map to others who have felt that same pull, to show that you are not imagining things, and to invite you on a journey that will alter what you believe possible.

If you are ready to step through, know this: you will not walk alone. Love is already waiting on the other side.

Chapter 9: How It Works

The method is simple, yet profound. It rests upon three foundations, the first of which is:

Opening the Doorway

Every journey begins with a threshold. You may think of it as a doorway between two rooms – one you know well, and one you have only glimpsed in dreams. To cross that threshold, you do not need to force anything, nor to summon powers you do not possess. You need only to remember.

Through story, through imagery, through presence, we begin to awaken the part of you that has always known how to walk between worlds. This is not about learning a new skill, nor about adopting beliefs you do not hold. It is about stirring what already lies dormant within you – the innate ability of your spirit to recognise and respond to the unseen.

As the doorway opens, your senses begin to shift. The ordinary becomes charged with something more. A word, a picture, a scent, a memory – any of these can act as a key, turning the lock and allowing the unseen to step forward. It is not fantasy. It is recognition. Your spirit leans forward, remembering a language it has never forgotten, though your mind may have silenced it.

When the doorway opens, you will know. The air will change. The weight of the room will alter, as though time itself has drawn a breath. You will feel yourself on the edge of something both familiar and mysterious, as if you are about to meet someone you have always known but have not yet remembered.

This is where the journey begins – not by escaping reality, but by expanding it. By opening to the truth that you are connected, always connected, to those who came before you, and that the doorway between worlds has never been locked, only waiting for you to step through.

Stepping Into the Story

Once the doorway opens, the journey begins to unfurl – not as something you watch from a distance, but as something you *enter*. You do not stand outside the story, peering through a window. You walk inside it. You breathe its air. You carry its weight.

You are no longer merely a witness. You are a participant.

You feel the emotions in your own body. A sudden grief grips your chest – but you realise it is not yours. Joy rises, unexpected and bright – but it belongs to another. Fear, longing, determination – each comes alive within you, flowing through your veins with a truth too vivid to dismiss. These are not shadows of the mind. They are the living imprints of those who came before you, pressing themselves gently, insistently, into your awareness.

At first, you may try to explain it away as imagination. But imagination is fragile – it flickers and fades when you question it. What unfolds here does not vanish. It deepens. It insists. It roots itself in you until you know, with certainty: *this is not pretend. This is real.*

You may find yourself standing in a kitchen you have never seen, yet everything is familiar. The smell of bread baking in an oven long extinguished wraps around you, warm and comforting. Or perhaps you feel the bone-deep weariness of a soldier returning from war, his boots heavy with mud, his heart heavy with things he cannot speak. You might step into the fierce resolve of a mother who kept her family alive through hunger and hardship, her determination now burning inside your own chest.

These are not tales you invent. They are echoes that reach across time, demanding to be remembered.

When you step into the story, you do not simply observe it – you *embody* it. You give voice to those who were silenced. You lend your tears to those who could not cry, your breath to those who could not speak, your laughter to those who had forgotten how. In carrying them, even for a moment, you bring them completion.

And within that act of embodiment lies the miracle: the power to heal.

Releasing and Returning

The final stage of the journey is release – the sacred act of laying down what has been carried in silence for too long. Generations may have held it close, hidden it away, unable or unwilling to give it voice. In The Loveday Method, those unspoken burdens are given space at last: space to be felt, honoured, and gently released.

As you move through the story, you may find yourself weeping the tears your grandmother was never permitted to shed. You may laugh aloud with the bubbling joy your uncle once held back, restrained by circumstance and sorrow. You may speak words that were caught in your ancestor's throat – words of longing, of anger, of love left unsaid. In that moment, you become the vessel through which their truth is finally expressed.

Now You Begin to Understand

Now that you have read these pages, you are beginning to understand why these stories were written. They may *sound* like fiction, because that is the safest way to present truths so vast, so luminous, that they might otherwise frighten or overwhelm. But the truth beneath them is clear: these stories are not invented. They are real.

They are written like tales, but they are not tales. They are maps. They are doorways. They are living threads connecting you to those who came before you, to places you have never been yet somehow remember, to voices that have been calling you all along.

Everything you have experienced so far – the images, the scents, the sensations, the sudden rushes of feeling – is part of that journey. It is so real that it becomes magical, and so magical that it reveals a deeper reality.

Now it is time. Time to remember who you are.

Beneath the noise of daily life, beneath the weight of inherited stories, beneath the layers of forgetting, there is a self within you that already knows this truth.

A self that recognises the faces of ancestors, that hears the songs of the unseen that remembers the love that cannot die.

These pages are not the end of the journey. They are the invitation. They are the moment when the veil lifts and you realise: you have always been more than a single lifetime, more than a single story.

You are a living continuation, a soul woven from countless threads, a being held by generations of love.

Now, as you turn the page, you do not simply read. You step through. You walk back into the river of memory and presence.

And as you do, you begin to remember who you truly are – and who has always been walking beside you.

And in giving their story its completion, something remarkable happens: the burden is lifted. The weight that pressed upon your lineage no longer rests upon your shoulders. It dissolves, not in rejection but in reverence, returned to the past where it belongs.

Then comes the return – the crossing back through the doorway into your own time, your own body, your own breath.

But you do not come back unchanged. You do not return empty. You return carrying a new clarity, a new spaciousness, a new freedom that ripples through every part of your life.

You discover that you have not left the past behind – you have brought its truth forward, woven into the present where it can heal and shine.

You emerge lighter, clearer, with the unshakable knowledge that you are not alone, that you walk within a lineage of love stretching far beyond what your eyes can see.

Release is never lost. Release is remembrance. By letting go of what was never truly yours, you create room for what has always been your birthright:

lightness, clarity, and the living presence of those who walk beside you still.

This is the gift of The Loveday Method: not only release, but return – a return to love, to connection, to the deepest knowing of who you are and where you come from.

Chapter 10: Into the Magic of Life

May these words not end here upon the page, but open within you like a lantern, casting light into forgotten corners of your soul. May you come to see that life itself is a story, threaded with mystery, alive with presence, shimmering with more than the eye can behold.

May you feel the quiet brush of your grandmother's hand in the stillness of morning? May you hear your uncle's laughter ripple through the silence when joy surprises you? May you sense your ancestors walking beside you when the path feels too heavy to walk alone?

This is the magic of life: that love never vanishes, that presence never dies, that the unseen waits patiently for us to remember. Every bird that lifts into flight, every breeze that stirs your cheek, every tear that falls unbidden is part of the great conversation – a reminder that you are held, guided, and cherished beyond measure.

When you close this book, do not imagine the journey is finished. It has only just begun. Step out into the world with new eyes, ready to notice the signs, the whispers, the echoes that have always been there. Step out knowing that every heartbeat is a doorway, every breath a bridge, every moment a chance to remember who you truly are.

So go now, with courage and tenderness. Walk into your days as though the whole of creation were leaning in to welcome you. For it is.

And so the journey begins – not away from life, but deeper into its magic.

Chapter 11: A Journey Through Time

Let me take you on a magical journey. You may be tempted to call it fiction, but I tell you now: the stories you are about to encounter are true. They live in the hidden folds of time, in the breath of memory, in the echoes that bind one life to another.

Our story begins in the year 1564 – the year William Shakespeare was born. Yet this tale is not about him. It was a time of brilliance, yes, but also of shadow, for disease swept through the land, leaving fear and grief in its wake. The world was alive with possibility, but it was also haunted by suffering.

Now let us move forward, as time folds upon itself like pages turning. The year is 1966.

Her name was Ann. She was young, yet her body was failing her in ways no one could explain. Doctors examined her, searched for answers, and came up empty. Her illness grew worse, but the cause remained a mystery. It was as though she carried something that did not belong solely to her – as though an invisible thread from another time had woven itself into her life.

What was this hidden weight she bore? What story was pressing through her body, demanding to be remembered?

The answers lie in the journey ahead.

Ann's Hidden Burden

The year was 1966. Ann was only twenty-two, yet her body felt twice that age. Her hands trembled, her breath often caught in her chest, and waves of exhaustion left her bedridden for days. She was examined by doctor after doctor, each more puzzled than the last. Tests revealed nothing. Treatments brought no relief.

Her family whispered among themselves – was it nerves, imagination, a weakness of the mind? But Ann knew what she felt was real. Something inside her was failing, and no one could explain why.

Yet beneath the physical decline was something more elusive, more haunting. At night, she dreamt of unfamiliar places. Narrow streets lined with timbered houses. A river that shimmered like liquid silver. And sometimes, faces she had never seen in her life – faces that seemed to know her.

One dream returned again and again: a woman, dressed in plain linen, lying pale and fevered upon a bed. The air smelled of sickness, the sound of coughing filled the room. Ann would wake from these dreams drenched in sweat, her own chest burning with pain.

She told no one, for how could she? Who would believe that her illness might belong not to her, but to another?

Her condition worsened. The doctors grew frustrated, her family frightened. And yet, in the midst of despair, there was a strange pull – as though the very illness was pointing somewhere, calling her to remember.

For the truth was this: Ann's body was carrying the echo of a life not her own. The fever, the weakness, the relentless decline – they were threads from another time, reaching through her blood, her bones, demanding recognition.

The year 1564 had not ended. It had lingered, alive within her.

Through The Loveday Method, this hidden burden would one day be brought to light. She would step into the life of the woman in her dreams, feel the fever that was never spoken of, hear the cries that went unanswered. And in doing so, she would release what her ancestor could not.

Ann's story is not simply about illness. It is about inheritance – the unseen legacies we carry, the griefs we live without knowing why. Her suffering was not a curse, but a message. A story waiting to be told.

And when it was finally spoken, the healing began.

Part 4:

Chapter 12: Ann's Journey

Case Study – Ann's Journey through a 6-session programme

When Ann came to see me, she was at her lowest ebb. Her body had become a stranger to her – weakening without reason, betraying her with exhaustion, fevers, and waves of pain that no physician could diagnose. She had visited clinics, endured endless tests, swallowed the medicines prescribed, yet none brought answers and none brought relief.

She was frightened, yes, but beyond fear lay something deeper: weariness. Ann was tired of carrying a burden she could not name, of living each day as though her body were speaking a language she could not translate.

And yet, beneath the despair, there flickered a quiet hope – the faint sense that her suffering must mean something, that it was not random, not cruel chance, but a message waiting to be heard.

From the very moment she stepped into the Loveday process, her body seemed to know what her mind had not yet grasped. Her breath deepened, her chest softened, and the tension in her face began to ease, as though a door within her had been waiting all this time to open. Something in her spirit recognised what was about to unfold, and welcomed it.

Ann was taken up a narrow flight of stairs, each step creaking as though carrying her deeper into a place both ancient and waiting. At the top, she saw a door. She described it in detail – an old wooden door, weathered by time, its grain darkened and worn smooth in places. In the centre was a round metal handle, dull with age but strong, gleaming faintly in the candlelight of her vision.

I told her gently: *"Once opened and passed through, this door will follow you wherever you go. If at any point you feel uneasy, you can return to it, step back through, and close it behind you. Whatever worries you carry will melt away the moment the door is shut."*

She nodded, her breath shallow. And then, slowly, she reached for the handle.

The doorway opened quickly for Ann, as though it had been waiting for her all along. The moment she crossed the threshold, she felt herself drop through time. Images rose with startling clarity, sharper than memory, more insistent than imagination.

She saw narrow cobbled streets, slick with rain. She heard the low rumble of wooden wheels and the sharp clatter of horse-drawn carts echoing between timbered houses. The air was damp, acrid, carrying the mingled scent of smoke, mud, and decay.

Ann described it aloud, her voice trembling, caught between awe and fear. *"It feels so real,"* she whispered, her breath quickening as though she were truly there.

And then came the dreams – the ones that had haunted her nights for months. But now they were not fragments, not half-remembered illusions. They opened before her like a curtain drawn aside.

She stood in a small, dim chamber. Shadows clung thick to the walls. The only light came from a single candle, its flame flickering in the stale air. The room reeked of sickness, metallic and sour.

On the bed lay a woman. Her skin was drained of colour, her body slick with sweat, her lips cracked and dry. A violent fever raged inside her, consuming her from within. Each breath rattled like a loose shutter in the wind – fragile, uneven, as though life itself was slipping from her.

Ann's whole body went rigid. Her hands flew to her mouth. Her eyes brimmed with tears. "It's her," she whispered, voice breaking. "The woman from my dreams."

In that moment, the boundary between memory and presence dissolved. Ann was no longer dreaming, nor merely imagining. She was standing at the threshold of another life – face-to-face with an echo that had crossed centuries to find her.

And then something shifted. The woman on the bed was no longer separate from her. Ann became her. She felt the heat, the weakness, the fear coursing through her own body.

The chamber, the fever, the failing breath – none of it belonged to Ann, yet all of it was alive within her. And she knew, with a certainty that needed no explanation, that this was the source of the weight she had carried her whole life.

The doorway had opened. And there was no turning back.

Ann's breathing grew shallow. Her body shook as she clutched her chest.

"It's inside me," she whispered. *"The fever – I can feel it. My skin is burning, but I'm cold all over. I can't... I can't breathe properly."*

Her voice quivered with terror. Her hands gripped the sides of the chair as though she were holding on for dear life.

I leaned closer, keeping my tone calm, grounding. *"Stay with it, Ann. You're safe here. What you're feeling is her story moving through you. Let it show itself. Don't fight it."*

Tears streamed down her cheeks. *"She's so afraid,"* she gasped. *"Not of dying – not exactly. She's afraid of leaving her children. She keeps looking at the door, waiting for them, hoping they'll come. She doesn't want to go. She's holding on for them."*

Ann's shoulders convulsed as sobs tore out of her. She pressed her palms to her eyes, as though to block the images, but they poured through her anyway. *"She's begging for just one more day. One more chance to hold them, to tell them she loves them."*

I placed a steady hand on her arm. *"Let her speak through you, Ann. Say the words she cannot say."*

Her lips trembled, then parted. In a broken voice, Ann cried out: *"I don't want to leave you! Please remember me. Don't forget me. I love you, I love you, I love you…"*

The words echoed into the room, raw and ancient, as though carried across centuries on Ann's breath.

Her body shuddered violently – then softened, as though something vast had been released. She sank back into her chair, tears flowing, chest rising and falling in long, relieved breaths.

"It's her sorrow," Ann whispered, quieter now, calmer. *"I've been carrying it all this time. The fear of being forgotten. The ache of leaving too soon. It wasn't mine – it was hers."*

I nodded gently. *"And now she has spoken. Through you, her story has been honoured. She does not need to hold it any longer – and neither do you."*

Ann closed her eyes. A look of peace spread across her face, fragile but real. She sat in silence for a long while, as though cradled by an invisible presence.

The room was still. It felt as if time itself had paused, bearing witness to a reunion and a release centuries overdue

At that moment, I gently guided Ann to separate from the body she had been inhabiting. The fevered woman's breath faded from her chest, and Ann returned to herself – her own body, her own voice, her own time. The weight of another's suffering began to ease, though its imprint lingered in the air around us.

"Now you are Ann again," I told her softly. *"That life has shown itself. But before it fades, I want you to look closely. Can you feel something in her story – a reflection, a mirror image – that connects to your own life? A feeling you have been carrying without knowing why?"*

Ann lay very still, her eyes fluttering beneath closed lids, her breath steady in the rhythm of trance. Slowly, she spoke.

"Yes…" Her voice was distant, dreamy. *"It's the same fear. The same weakness. I've always felt fragile, as if my body could collapse without reason. No one could explain it. The doctors never knew. It was her. I've been carrying her illness… her sorrow."*

Her brow furrowed. *"And the loneliness… She felt so alone when she died. I know that feeling. Even in a room full of people, I feel like no one sees me. Like I'll be forgotten."*

Her words cracked, her voice breaking under the weight of recognition.

I spoke gently, guiding her deeper: *"Yes, Ann. Those feelings – the weakness in your body, the loneliness in your heart – they are not yours alone. They have been passed to you, carried across time. But you do not have to hold them forever. Do you understand?"*

A single tear slipped from her closed eyes. *"Yes. I understand. They're not mine."*

The silence that followed was thick, sacred. Ann's body trembled once, then stilled, as if releasing something that had been woven into her for too long.

She whispered, almost inaudible: *"She can rest now. And so can I."*

Releasing and Returning

I spoke softly, my voice steady and calm. *"Ann,"* I said, *"repeat after me."*

Her lips parted, her eyes still closed, her body trembling as if on the edge of something vast.

Slowly, haltingly, she spoke the words aloud:

"I will honour your memory, but I cannot relive your life. The sadness, the fear, the unhappiness, the loneliness, the fear of losing my children is not mine. The insecurities are yours. All these feelings I have been holding onto – I return them to you now."

As the final words left her mouth, a shudder ran through Ann's body. Her hands clenched, then relaxed. Her head tilted back as if a weight were being lifted.

She gasped. *"Something's leaving me…"*

I watched her closely. Her face was pale but serene, her breath deep and slow. She whispered, *"It's dark… like smoke… it's leaving my chest. Going back to her."*

In that moment, Ann was not only healing herself; she was healing the woman whose suffering she had carried. The story had been witnessed, spoken, and now it could be returned.

Tears slid down her cheeks, but her voice was clear: *"It was never my fault. I was not to blame."*

Then she stilled, eyes fluttering behind her lids. *"I can see threads..."* she murmured.

"Tell me about them," I prompted gently.

"They're cotton," she said after a pause. *"Soft, but strong. They stretch from her to me."*

"And what do you wish to do with them?"

"Cut them," she breathed.

"Then cut them now. Cut them in your mind. Release them."

Her right hand lifted slightly, palm open. She described a beam of light forming there – a narrow, brilliant line, sharp as a blade, humming with power.

"I'm cutting them," she whispered. *"One by one... they're snapping... unravelling..."*

She inhaled sharply, then nodded, her head bowing as though in reverence.

"They're gone. The connection is gone."

She grew quiet. Her shoulders lowered, her body softened.

"Now there's a web..." she said at last. "A spider's web of threads... so many lives, all connected from the past to the present... like a bridge of time. But the light is cutting them, too. The beam moves through my palm. They're dissolving."

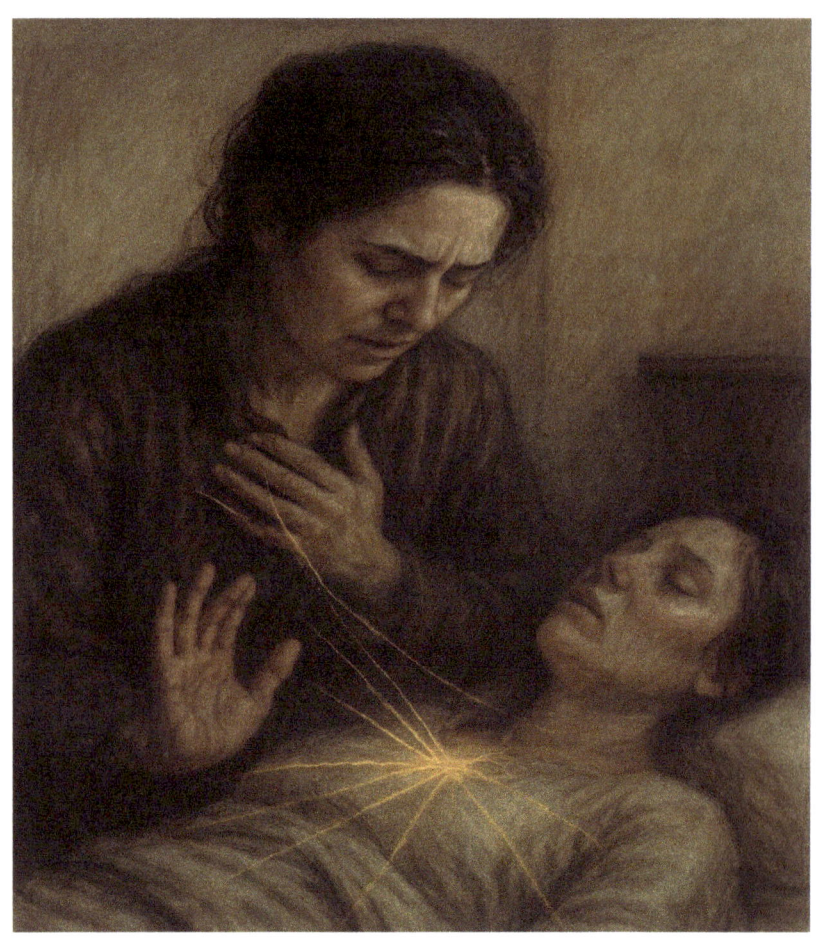

Her eyes fluttered open briefly, a small smile trembling at her lips. *"It's done. It's all gone."*

The room felt still, yet charged with a quiet, luminous energy – as if both Ann and her ancestor had been released at once.

The Light of Peace

At that moment, the universe itself seemed to open.

A rainbow of colours descended like a waterfall of light, each hue shimmering with its own vibration – deep indigo and violet, radiant gold, emerald green, rose pink, sapphire blue. They floated down and surrounded them both – Ann and the ancestor she had carried – enveloping them in a sphere of pure radiance.

Ann's body relaxed into the glow. Her breath deepened as she drew the light into herself. With each inhalation, the colours streamed through her, moving in gentle waves, recharging every chakra in her body.

She described the sensations as they unfolded:

"The crown of my head is tingling... there's warmth in my chest... my stomach feels lighter... my whole body is filled with light."

The rainbow bathed her from crown to root, aligning, balancing, restoring. Her hands unclenched, her shoulders dropped, her lips curved into the faintest smile.

Then, with a quiet sob that was not sorrow but relief, she whispered: *"I feel love. It's in me. It's been here all along."*

Strength pulsed through her body – not a sharp rush, but a steady, grounded power. For the first time in years, she felt not frail, not broken, but whole.

And with that strength came peace. A peace so deep it silenced the mind, stilled the heart, and wrapped her in a presence beyond words.

Ann opened her eyes at last, shining with tears yet radiant, transformed. *"For the first time,"* she said softly, *"I feel peace."*

I asked Ann to close her eyes once more and speak the words aloud, letting them rise from her heart into the space between her and the woman she had carried.

Softly, through trembling lips, she repeated after me:

"I forgive you. Because by forgiving you, I set us both free. I forgive you, because the cords have been cut. I forgive you, because now we can both find peace."

Her voice cracked, but she did not falter. The words filled the air, vibrating with a truth older than time.

"Ann," I said gently, *"when you look into her eyes now, what do you feel?"*

Ann's lips curved into a trembling smile. *"Love,"* she whispered.

"And when she looks into your eyes, what does she see?"

Ann's tears glistened as they fell. *"She feels love too."*

At that moment, a radiant light enveloped her – soft, shimmering, golden. It wrapped around her like a cloak, filling the room with a quiet brilliance. She gasped softly. *"It's beautiful,"* she said. *"She's surrounding me with love."*

"What is she trying to tell you?" I asked.

Ann's voice grew steadier, clearer, infused with a strength she had never spoken with before. *"She's telling me… it's time to live my life."*

And then, as though the veil between worlds had thinned to transparency, Ann saw them – not just the woman she had carried, but others too. Her ancestors gathered behind her, a multitude of faces, some familiar, some unknown, all radiant. They were smiling, waving, their eyes shining with pride.

"They're here," Ann whispered in awe. "They're waving to me."

I nodded, my own heart stirred. "Yes, Ann. They are proud of you. And they will be watching over you, always."

The chamber of suffering dissolved. In its place was light, presence, and the unmistakable bond of love that death could never sever. Ann sat quietly, breathing in her newfound peace, held by the ancestors who had waited for this moment – not only her healing, but theirs.

I spoke softly to Ann. *"Now, Ann, begin to walk towards the door. There is a gift waiting there –*

something left only for you. Only you will understand what it means."

She moved slowly, her eyes still closed but her breath steady, as if she could see it as clearly as daylight. *"By the side of the door,"* she murmured, *"there's a box…"*

"Describe it to me," I prompted gently.

"It's dark oak," she whispered. *"Heavy, old… but beautiful. It feels like it's been waiting for me."*

"Open it when you're ready," I said.

Her hands trembled slightly. She inhaled deeply, then described lifting the lid. Inside lay a single folded note, yellowed with age, the edges soft and worn.

She opened it and began to read aloud:

"You are never alone. You are loved by so many. We are so proud of you."

Tears streamed down Ann's cheeks. Her voice caught as she read.

"Who do you feel left this note for you?" I asked quietly.

"My grandmother..." Ann breathed. "I never got over losing her. I was seven when she died."

I waited a moment, then said softly, "Would you like to know who truly sent it?"

Ann nodded, whispering, "Yes. Please."

"Then hold the note in front of you," I told her. "The person who wrote it will appear."

Her fingers curled around the paper. The air in the room seemed to shift. Ann's breath caught, then she gasped.

"She's here..." she whispered. "My grandmother... She's here."

In her vision, the figure of a woman stepped forward from the shadows. Ann's face crumpled. "It's her... it's really her..."

They moved towards each other and embraced. Ann sobbed softly as she described the feeling of arms around her – warm, firm, unmistakable. She inhaled deeply. *"Her perfume..."* she murmured. *"The same scent she wore. It's real. She's real."*

This was not a memory. It was not my imagination. It was a reunion.

Ann clung to her grandmother as though she were seven again, yet stronger now, knowing the truth of what she was experiencing. In that embrace she felt the love she had missed for so long, a love that had never left her, a love that had waited patiently for this moment.

At last, I asked Ann to turn her attention once more to the door.

"Tell me, Ann," I said gently, *"what colour is the door now?"*

She paused, her lips parting as though in awe. *"It's white,"* she whispered. *"Pure, perfect white."*

"And what does that mean to you?"

Her voice grew stronger, steady with certainty. *"It means... a new beginning."*

With that, she placed her hand upon the handle and slowly opened the door. Beyond it was not the shadowed chamber of sickness, but a space radiant with light. She stepped through. With reverence, she closed the door behind her.

I asked her to walk back down the stairs. This time the steps glowed beneath her feet, lit as though by hidden lanterns. The sunlight streamed all around her, flooding every corner, illuminating her path.

When she reached the bottom, I began to guide her gently back. Counting softly to five, I drew her from the journey and back into the present.

At the count of five, Ann opened her eyes.

The change was immediate, undeniable. Her eyes shone – vibrant, alive, alight with health and energy. The heaviness that had shadowed her face for so long had lifted. In its place was clarity, lightness, and a quiet radiance that spoke of renewal.

This was not the end. There were five further sessions to follow, each one opening new doorways, each one unravelling more of the burden she had carried. But this moment was the beginning – the first step into freedom, the first glimpse of who Ann could be without the weight of another's suffering upon her.

It was the birth of a new life.

And Ann, for the first time in many years, was ready to live it.

Chapter 13: Preparing for the Second Journey – Beyond the Veil

When Ann returned a week later, her eyes already carried a spark of the light she had discovered in her first session. Before I began the induction, I explained carefully what she was about to experience, so she would feel safe and ready to let go.

"Ann," I said softly, "this time, you will be taken deeper. You will climb a set of stairs – or perhaps descend them. Your spirit will choose the way. At the top, or at the bottom, you will find a door. This door does not belong to one place or one time – it is a doorway that opens into another time.

"Beside the door, you will notice a rainbow of colours. Step into the rainbow. Allow it to surround you, to flow through you, to enter your body. Let it heal you, strengthen you, restore balance.

"Once you are bathed in this light, you will begin to rise. Higher and higher. You may see mountains below you, snow upon the peaks, birds wheeling through the air. You may rise above the clouds, where the sky deepens to indigo and the sun's golden rays warm your face.

"And then, Ann, you will rise beyond our universe, into the unknown, a place called the emptiness. There, you will find another doorway – vast and shimmering. When you step through, silence will greet you, a stillness without weight. This is the place where past lives are laid to rest, where the ancestors wait.

"In that stillness, you may notice threads stretching through time – weaving from past to present, from one life to another. One thread will call to you. It may glow, it may pull at you, and you will know it is the one that has been touching your life now.

"When you follow it, you will see an ancestor – male or female, perhaps shifting between the two – and in their reflection you will recognise the feelings you have been carrying: sadness, loneliness, fear.

"When that happens, you will have the chance to give it back. You will open your palms, and with your breath you will release those feelings into the vastness. You will know with certainty that they are not yours. And in that moment, Ann, you will not only heal yourself – you will also free the one who came before you."

I let the words settle between us. Ann's breath deepened as she listened, her eyes already softening. She nodded gently, as if her spirit recognised the path before her.

The Island of Light

"At that moment, Ann, the doorway will open and you will step through, continuing your journey. On the other side, a vision will unfold before you: a beautiful island, radiant and untouched, surrounded by clear waters that sparkle in the sunlight. The air will be fresh, scented with flowers, and the ground beneath your feet will feel warm and alive.

Here, upon this sacred island, we will begin the opening of your chakras. One by one, each centre of energy within your body will awaken and come into balance.

At the crown of your head, a soft violet light will descend, connecting you to the vastness of the universe. At your brow, an indigo flame will kindle, sharpening your vision and guiding your inner wisdom. At your throat, a pure blue radiance will flow, freeing your voice and your truth. At your heart, a gentle green light will open, filling you with love, compassion, and peace. At your solar plexus, a golden sun will glow, restoring your strength, your confidence, your power. At your navel, a warm orange energy will ripple outward, bringing joy, creativity, and flow. And at the base of your spine, a deep red root will steady and ground you, anchoring you safely to the earth.

As these lights open and align, the island itself will seem to glow with you. You will feel the rainbow of energy flowing through your body, recharging every part of you, until you are whole, balanced, and strong."

Into the Deep Trance

I invited Ann to close her eyes and let her breath fall into an easy rhythm. With each exhalation her body grew heavier, and with each inhalation her mind became lighter, more open, and more free.

I counted softly, drawing her deeper and deeper, until her body was still and her spirit awake. She was safe, relaxed, and ready.

And then I guided her to step across the threshold into her magical journey.

What follows is her story – not imagination, not invention, but the living experience that unfolded before her:

Ann's Journey – In Her Own Words

"I'm standing at the bottom of the stairs now… they look old, stone steps, but they're glowing faintly, as if light is guiding me upward.

I'm walking slowly... step by step. I feel lighter with each movement, like something is lifting away from me as I climb.

I see a door at the top. It's very old... wooden, heavy, with a round metal handle in the centre. It looks as though it has been waiting just for me.

I can feel the coolness of the handle beneath my fingers. I'm turning it... the door is opening...

Oh... colours... a rainbow of colours is spilling out, flowing around me, wrapping me in light. Red, orange, gold, green, blue, indigo, violet... they're entering my body, filling every space inside me.

My chest feels warm, my head feels clear, my whole body is humming. It's healing me. Balancing me. Making me strong."

(Pause – a deeper breath, her voice softens.)

"I'm rising now… floating upwards. The ground is falling away beneath me. I can see mountains, the snow glittering white on their peaks. Birds are circling, soaring, calling out to one another. The air is cold and fresh against my skin.

I'm moving higher, above the clouds. The sky is deep blue, almost indigo. The sun's rays are pouring into me, golden, filling my chest with warmth. It's like breathing in pure light. I feel so free."

(A whisper, awed.)

"I've gone beyond the clouds now… beyond the earth itself. There are stars everywhere. Bright, endless stars. The darkness is vast but it isn't frightening. It's beautiful… still… eternal. I feel very small, but at the same time… completely held."

(Her voice trembles, a hush of reverence.)

"There's a doorway ahead of me... it's enormous, glowing, with no clear edges. Just pure shimmering light. I'm stepping through... the doorway closes behind me... and now I'm in emptiness. A vast stillness. It's quiet, but alive.

This is where all the past lives are resting... all the ancestors. I can sense them. So many. They're here with me."

(A sharp intake of breath. Her brow furrows.)

"I can see threads... thousands of them, like a great weaving. They stretch through time, connecting life to life, past to present. One thread is glowing brighter... it's pulling at me. Heavy. It hurts. I feel its weight in my chest.

It's sadness. Loneliness. Fear. It feels like it belongs to me – but no, no... it's older. It's an ancestor. Male? Female? The image shifts, but the emotions are the same. They've been carrying despair. And I've been carrying it too."*

(She gasps, tears breaking free.)

"It's not mine... I've been living with it all this time, thinking it was me, but it's not. It's theirs. I don't need to hold it anymore. I'm giving it back. I'm giving all of it back – the sadness, the fear, the loneliness. It's not mine."

(Her voice strengthens as she exhales, releasing.)

"Oh... it's leaving me. I can feel it. Like smoke lifting out of my chest. It's going back to them. It's dissolving. I'm lighter... freer. And they're lighter too. They're free."

(Silence, then a deep, steady breath. Her tone changes – gentle, radiant.)

"Now there's light... so much light. A rainbow again, flowing into me. Filling me. My whole body is alive with it. My heart feels open, warm, full of love. I feel strong. I feel safe.

For the first time... I feel peace."

Ann's Journey – The Island of Red Light

"At that moment… another doorway opens. It's like a frame of shimmering light, and I'm drawn to it. I step through. The door closes softly behind me, like a sigh, and I'm somewhere entirely new.

I'm travelling… moving forward… and now I see an island. It's glowing ahead of me, surrounded by water so clear it looks like glass. I walk down from the light and step onto the earth.

I'm in a valley… oh, it's beautiful… trees rising tall and green, flowers everywhere, waterfalls tumbling from rocks, their mist cool on my face. The air is fresh and sweet. Everything feels alive here.

And now… it's changing. The colours are shifting. The valley is filling with red – the most beautiful shades of red I've ever seen. Crimson, ruby, scarlet, deep rose. It isn't frightening; it's warm, powerful. It surrounds me, it enters me.

The red light is flowing into my body. I can feel it in my base, at the root of my spine. It's like a glowing ember becoming a flame, brighter and brighter. My legs feel strong, my feet steady. The red light is recharging my root chakra, making me solid, grounded, safe.

It's pulsing now… brighter… brighter… until I feel like I'm standing in the heart of the earth itself. My whole lower body feels anchored and alive, filled with strength I didn't know I had. I'm safe. I'm rooted. I belong."

"At that moment... another doorway opens. It's like a frame of shimmering light, and I'm drawn to it. I step through. The door closes softly behind me, like a sigh, and I'm somewhere entirely new.

I'm travelling... moving forward... and now I see an island. It's glowing ahead of me, surrounded by water so clear it looks like glass. I walk down from the light and step onto the earth.

I'm in a valley... oh, it's beautiful... trees rising tall and green, flowers everywhere, waterfalls tumbling from rocks, their mist cool on my face. The air is fresh and sweet. Everything feels alive here.

And now... it's changing. The colours are shifting. The valley is filled with red – the most beautiful shades of red I've ever seen. Crimson, ruby, scarlet, deep rose. It isn't frightening; it's warm, powerful. It surrounds me, it enters me.

The red light is flowing into my body. I can feel it in my base, at the root of my spine. It's like a glowing ember becoming a flame, brighter and brighter. My legs feel strong, my feet steady. The red light is recharging my root chakra, making me solid, grounded, safe.

It's pulsing now... brighter... brighter... until I feel like I'm standing in the heart of the earth itself. My whole lower body feels anchored and alive, filled with strength I didn't know I had. I'm safe. I'm rooted. I belong."

Ann's Journey – The Valley of Orange Light

"The red is fading now... softening... shifting. Oh... now it's changing. The whole valley is filled with orange

– the most beautiful, glowing orange. It's warm, rich, like sunset poured into the air. It surrounds me, it flows into me.

I can feel it entering just above the root, in my lower belly… the sacral chakra. It's glowing inside me, soft and bright.

It feels like warmth in water… like waves moving gently through me. It's playful, creative. I feel a joy rising in me I haven't felt in years… the kind of joy that makes you laugh for no reason.

The orange light is filling me with flow, with movement. It's telling me it's safe to feel, safe to create, safe to enjoy. My whole lower body is alive, glowing, radiant.

It's beautiful… it's glowing brighter and brighter… my sacral centre is lit, like a flame dancing happily inside me."

Ann's Journey – The Valley of Yellow Light

"The orange is softening now... dissolving... and it changes again. The whole valley is filled with yellow – the most beautiful yellows I've ever seen. Bright like sunlight, soft like buttercups, golden like fields of wheat.

It streams into me, filling my body, and it comes to rest at my solar plexus – the third chakra, just below my ribs. Oh... it's glowing there, warm, steady, alive.

It feels like a sun inside me, a golden flame. It's strong, but not harsh – it's steady, confident, powerful. The yellow light is reminding me who I am, that I have strength, that I have purpose.

I feel my centre glowing brighter and brighter, like I could stand tall against anything. The yellow fills me with courage, with clarity. I feel awake, alive, and powerful in the best way.

It's so bright now – a golden sun within me – shining out into the world."

Ann's Journey – The Valley of Green Light

"The yellow is softening... fading like a sunset, and now... oh, it's changing again. The whole valley is turning green – the most beautiful shades of green I've ever seen. Emerald, jade, soft moss, fresh spring leaves. It's everywhere, surrounding me, flowing into me.

It enters my chest, right into the centre of my heart. The fourth chakra... the heart chakra.

Oh... it's glowing. I can feel it spreading through my chest, soft but so powerful. It feels like unconditional love, pouring through me. Love that doesn't ask, doesn't judge, doesn't end.

It's warm... it's soft... it's limitless. My whole chest is open, glowing with green light. I can feel it reaching out beyond me, touching everything, everyone.

The green light is teaching me that love is always here, that I *am* love. My heart is glowing brighter and brighter, radiating peace, kindness, compassion.

I feel open. I feel whole. I feel loved."

Ann's Journey – The Valley of Blue Light

"The green is softening now... gently dissolving like mist. And the colours are changing again. Oh... it's turning blue – the most beautiful blues I've ever seen. Clear like the summer sky, deep like the ocean, shimmering like sapphires. The whole valley is filled with blue.

It enters my body, flowing straight into my throat, my fifth chakra. I can feel it spinning there, glowing, and opening.

It's like a cool breeze, refreshing, clearing away all the heaviness that was caught in my voice. I feel as though I can breathe more easily, as if my words are freer. The blue light is cleansing me, washing through me, giving me permission to speak.

I can feel the times I silenced myself, the times I swallowed words I longed to say. They're loosening now, releasing. The blue is telling me: *'Your voice matters. Your truth matters. Speak it. Sing it. Share it.'*

Oh, it's glowing brighter... brighter... my whole throat is alive with blue light. I feel clear, expressive, and open.

It feels like I could sing my soul into the world."

Ann's Journey – The Indigo Light

"The blue is softening now... fading like waves pulling back into the sea. And the colours are shifting once more. Oh... now it's indigo. The most beautiful indigo light – deep, velvety, endless. It's like midnight skies full of stars, like the stillness of twilight, like the mysteries of the universe wrapped in one colour. The whole valley is glowing with indigo.

It enters my forehead, between my brows – my third eye chakra. Oh... I can feel it glowing there, pulsing gently, opening. It's as if a window has been thrown wide inside my mind.

The indigo light is clear but vast, like stepping into infinity. I can see so much more than before – not with my eyes, but with something deeper. My intuition is alive, my inner knowing is awake.

Visions are flickering through me – glimpses of the past, echoes of lives long gone, threads weaving into the present. It's all connected. I understand now: nothing is separate. Every choice, every soul, every life is woven together.

The indigo light whispers to me: *'Trust what you see. Trust what you feel. Your wisdom is already within you.'*

It's glowing brighter, brighter... my whole mind feels illuminated, expanded. I feel as though I can see through time itself, beyond the surface of life, into the heart of truth.

I am awake. I am aware. I am connected."

Ann's Journey – The Violet Crown

"The indigo is softening now... dissolving into stillness. And above me... oh... a new colour is descending. Violet. The most beautiful violet light, shimmering with hints of silver and white. It's like starlight made into colour, like the petals of a lotus opening at dawn, like the universe pouring itself into me.

The violet light is entering the crown of my head, my seventh chakra. I feel it flowing down like a fountain, streaming into me, moving through every part of my body. My whole being is filled with it.

It's weightless, infinite... yet it makes me feel completely whole. I can sense the divine – not out there somewhere far away, but here, inside me, around me, everywhere.

Oh... it's as though I am dissolving into light. My boundaries are melting. I am not just Ann, I am everything. I am part of the stars, part of the earth, part of every soul who has ever lived. I can feel the presence of the universe holding me, loving me, flowing through me.

The violet light is telling me: *'You are never alone. You have always been one with us. You are loved beyond measure.'*

It's growing brighter, brighter, until it feels as though my whole body is radiant, glowing like pure light. I feel expanded, limitless, free.

This is peace beyond peace. This is love beyond love. This is home."

Ann's Journey – Entering the Rainbow

"You're telling me I have the power to change the world... and as you say it, something happens inside me. Oh... oh my goodness... all the colours of the rainbow are seeping out of my skin. I can see them, I can feel them. They're pouring from me like light, streaming into the air.

Everything around me is changing... the sky... the trees... even the wings of butterflies fluttering past. They're all becoming rainbows – shimmering bands of colour, blending into one another, more beautiful than anything I've ever seen. Crimson into gold, sapphire into emerald, rose into violet. The whole world is glowing.

It's so vivid... so alive... I can almost hear the colours singing.

You're speaking to me now about the pot of gold at the end of the rainbow. You're saying that for everyone it's different – a message, a letter, a person, an intuition – and only I will know its meaning.

I understand. I can feel it. This is my path, my sign.

I'm looking now… following the rainbow. It stretches out before me like a living bridge. The colours are dancing, rippling, calling me forward.

I'm moving towards it, step by step. The ground beneath my feet glows with each step I take. The rainbow is drawing me in, as though it wants me to find its end.

Oh… there it is. The end of the rainbow. It's not an end at all – it's a doorway made of light, colours swirling endlessly into each other.

I'm standing right in front of it now. It's humming, alive, waiting for me.

I'm reaching out my hand. The light is warm against my skin. It feels like home.

I'm stepping in. The colours wrap around me, through me, like liquid light. I'm entering the rainbow itself. Everything is glowing… everything is one…"

Ann's Journey – The Gift in the Rainbow

"I'm inside the rainbow now. The colours aren't just around me, they're inside me – flowing through my veins, filling every part of me. It feels like floating in warm water made of light. There's no weight, no edge… only colour, sound, and a feeling of being completely held.

Something's ahead of me… it's forming out of the colours. It's a shape… no, a box… but it's glowing. It's not like a box you open with your hands, it's more like a heart opening.

It's waiting for me.

You're telling me there's a message, a gift for me. I reach towards it and it opens, and a wave of light comes out – golden, soft, shimmering like starlight.

Inside the light is a note. It's so clear I can read it without touching it. It says:

'Live, Ann. Live your life. All that you've carried is done. You are free, you are loved, you are guided. Go forward.'

I'm crying. The tears are warm, but they're happy tears. My chest feels wide open. The message is sinking into me, deeper than words.

And now... oh... someone's here. The light is taking shape again. It's my grandmother. I know it instantly – the smell of her perfume, the warmth of her arms. She's smiling at me. We're hugging. It's real. It's not a memory. It's reunion.

She's whispering to me: *'We're all so proud of you. You're never alone.'*

I feel her hands on my shoulders. I feel strong. I feel loved. The rainbow around us glows brighter and brighter, as if every ancestor is there, watching, smiling, waving me on.

The gift... the real gift... is knowing I am free to live my life now. I'm not carrying anyone else's sorrow. I'm living for me, and they're all behind me, loving me, cheering me forward."

Ann's Journey – Returning to the World

"The rainbow is softening now... fading around me like a sunset. I'm turning away, slowly, gently, and I start to walk back towards the light I came in through. My steps feel lighter than air.

I'm rising up... the doorway is opening ahead of me. I step through and the rainbow dissolves behind me. The doorway closes. Now I'm in a vast, quiet emptiness. It's not lonely. It's peace. Everything is still, like a great silent heartbeat holding me.

Another doorway is opening... pure light. I walk through, and when it closes, I'm back in our universe. The darkness is soft and deep, scattered with stars. They're everywhere – bright, sparkling, alive. The stars look like lanterns, like eyes of love watching over me.

I'm moving through space now. I can see the Earth turning slowly, colours blending together perfectly – oceans and clouds, greens and blues swirling as one. It's beautiful... so beautiful.

And now every star in the universe is pouring love and light into me. I can feel it rushing through me – golden, silver, violet – filling every cell. I'm glowing. I'm a star myself. Part of everything. I can feel the whole universe inside me, and me inside it.

I'm travelling back now, gently, calmly. The light of the stars is still in me. I'm descending toward the Earth, coming closer, closer.

I step out of the light. I see the door again, and the stairs where I started. Everything looks the same, yet brighter, clearer. I feel new.

I'm walking down the stairs slowly, and with each step I feel more grounded, more present. My feet are on the earth.

You're counting now... one... two... three... four... five... and as you say five, I open my eyes.

Oh... what a change.

Everything feels lighter. My body feels alive. My eyes are clear, vibrant. I can feel the light still in me, as though I'm carrying the stars back into the world. I'm here... but I'm different. I'm home."

Chapter 14: The Third Session – The Akashic Library

A week later Ann arrived for her third session. Already there was a new softness in her face, a steadiness in her step. The light she had carried from the previous journeys still glimmered in her eyes.

Before beginning, I explained what she would encounter this time:

"Ann," I said softly, "today we will go somewhere different. It is not a valley or an island, but a place of knowledge – a library that holds the stories of all souls. Some call it the Akashic Library. It is vast, silent, and timeless. In its halls are the records of every life that has ever been lived, every thought, every choice, every possibility.

"When you arrive there, you may see it as an endless hall of books, or scrolls, or lights – your spirit will choose how to show it to you. You may be drawn to a single book, or to a table, or to a guide waiting for you. Whatever appears, it is safe. It is for you.

"This library will not overwhelm you. It will offer only what you are ready to receive. And if at any time you wish to step back, the door will be there waiting – the same door as before, ready to bring you home."

Ann listened with her eyes closed, her hands resting loosely on her knees. She nodded once, slowly, a sign of readiness. Her breath had already deepened; she was slipping into the quiet before trance.

"Now," I said gently, "close your eyes and let the journey begin. You will climb or descend the stairs again. You will find the door. When you pass through it this time, you will enter the Akashic Library."

Ann's Journey – The Akashic Library

"I'm climbing the stairs again... each step lighter, easier. The door is waiting for me. The round handle is cool in my hand... I'm opening it now.

I step through and – oh... this is different. I'm not in a valley, not in colours. I'm in a vast hall. It stretches forever in every direction.

There are shelves rising higher than I can see. Endless shelves. They're filled with books – thousands, millions, more than I can count. Some glow faintly, as though they're alive. The air feels hushed, holy, like a great cathedral of knowledge.

I'm walking slowly. My footsteps echo on the floor. It's smooth, polished stone. Everything is still, but not empty. I can feel presences here, quiet but watchful, almost like librarians. Guides. They don't speak, but they nod, as though they've been expecting me.

I reach out to a shelf... my hand stops on a book. It's thick, bound in leather, warm to the touch. It's glowing faintly, just for me. I open it.

Oh… these aren't words like I know them. They're images, colours, feelings. They move across the page like living memories.

I see a life… It feels familiar. A woman, long ago. She's carrying so much sorrow. It's her story… but it's also mine. The book is showing me the thread that runs from her into me.

I can feel my chest tightening, but then the page shifts. Light pours across it. The sorrow is acknowledged, honoured, and then dissolves.

I turn to another page. This time I see possibilities… paths I could walk. Futures branching out like rivers from a single source. One is glowing brighter, warmer. I know it's the one I'm meant to follow. It feels like freedom.

The book is telling me something: *'You are not bound by the past. You are guided by it, but you are free.'*

I close the book gently. It feels complete.

The guides are smiling now. They don't need to speak. I can feel their approval, their blessing.

The library is fading. The shelves are dissolving into light. I know I can return here whenever I need. The door is appearing again. I'm stepping through, carrying the wisdom with me."

Ann's Journey – The Chair and the Drop Through Time

"I'm still in the library... walking slowly. And there – oh – there's a chair. A very old chair. It's heavy, leather worn soft by so many who have sat in it before. It feels like it's been waiting for me. I'm drawn to it. I have to sit down.

I'm lowering myself into the chair now. The leather is cool, smooth, and comforting. As soon as I sit, something happens... I feel myself sinking... falling... as though the chair is a doorway itself.

I'm dropping through time.

Oh... everything is changing. The light, the air, the sounds. I hear distant hoofbeats, voices in another accent. My chest feels tight. I know... it's 1865.

I see headlines, whispers of history... it was the time Abraham Lincoln was assassinated. The world feels raw, unsettled.

I look down at my hands. They're not mine. They're strong, calloused, but the colour is dark. My skin is dark. My clothes are coarse, worn. My body is different. I'm someone else.

I can feel emotions rising – fear, grief, confusion. They're not mine. They belong to the life I've stepped into. All this time, I've been holding onto these feelings without knowing. They've been flowing into me from this life… but they're not mine."

Ann's Journey – The Weight of Injustice

"I can feel it more clearly now. The year is 1865… the air is thick with unrest. The streets are loud with talk – Lincoln has been killed, and with him, hope feels fragile, shaken.

I see myself in another body, another skin. My hands are rough, darkened, scarred by labour. My back aches with the memory of years bent in toil. I was born into chains. Even when they said freedom had come, it did not feel like freedom. There was fear in every breath.

I remember the sound of boots – heavy, cruel. The way voices could turn sharp, dangerous, in an instant. I remember the eyes that would not meet mine, as though I were invisible, less than human. The names shouted, the threats whispered, the rights denied.

And the sorrow... oh, the sorrow of families torn apart. Mothers clutching children, afraid of losing them. Husbands hiding, wives waiting. People branded by skin, by birth, by something they never chose.

I can feel the anger in my blood – anger that had no safe place to go. I can feel the grief that sank deep into my bones, the hopelessness of living as though life itself were a crime.

It's all pressing down on me now... but I know, I know these feelings are not mine. They are his. They are theirs. They are the echoes of a life lived in injustice.

I breathe deeply. My chest is shaking, but I whisper: *'I see it. I know what you endured. I honour it. But I cannot carry it. It is not mine.'*

Slowly, haltingly, I speak the words aloud: *'I will honour your memory, but I cannot relive your life. The sadness, the fear, the unhappiness, the loneliness, the fear of losing my children is not mine. The insecurities are yours. All these feelings I have been holding onto – I return them to you now.'*

As the last words leave my lips, the weight begins to lift. The grief rises like a dark cloud, dissolving into the air. The fear loosens its grip. The anger softens, melts into something quieter.

What remains is his strength – the unbroken spirit, the courage that no cruelty could erase. That flows into me now, bright and steady, like fire that cannot be put out.

I whisper again, through tears: *'You are remembered. You are free. And so am I.'*

He is fading, turning to light… but his dignity stays with me, strong and unshakable. The injustice dissolves, but the soul lives on – proud, whole, eternal."

Ann's Journey – The Threads of Time

"He is fading now, turning into light… but as he dissolves, I begin to see something else. Threads. Thousands of them, fine and shimmering, stretching out in every direction. They are woven like a vast web across existence itself.

They connect the past to the present – a bridge through time. Each thread carries the weight of a story, a memory, an emotion. Some glisten with love, with joy, with strength. Others are darker, heavy with grief, fear, or silence.

I can see how they weave into me, into my own life, binding me to things I never lived, yet always felt. It's like walking across a bridge built from the experiences of those who came before me.

Some of the threads pulse faintly, asking to be honoured. Others tug, tight and insistent, asking to be released.

And in my hands now, I feel light. Pure light, sharp and strong, flowing from my palms like a beam. I understand… This is the tool. This is what I must use.

With reverence, I raise my hand. The beam of light extends, and as it touches a thread heavy with sorrow, the cord dissolves, melting into gold dust that drifts away.

Another thread appears – loneliness, not mine but carried within me. I lift my hand again, and with a sweep of light, I cut it. The tension vanishes. I feel the release move through my chest, my heart.

One by one, I free them. The web shimmers, changing, and lightening. The threads that remain glow brighter, radiant with love and wisdom. The others fall away, their burdens no longer bound to me, nor to those who will come after me.

I am not breaking the past. I am healing it. I am not severing love. I am releasing pain.

And with each thread that dissolves, I feel lighter, clearer, more alive. The bridge through time still stands – but now it carries only love."

Ann's Journey – Wrapped in the Rainbow

"The last of the heavy threads has dissolved now. The web is still here, but it's glowing – lighter, clearer, shining with only love.

And then... oh... something is happening. Colours... the most beautiful colours are pouring towards me. A rainbow, alive and moving, flowing from the web, from the universe, from everywhere at once.

The colours surround me, circling me like ribbons of light. Red, orange, yellow, green, blue, indigo, violet – each one weaving around me, through me, filling every part of me.

The red flows into my base, steadying me, grounding me like roots deep in the earth. The orange warms my belly, filling me with joy, creativity, flow. The yellow glows in my centre, bright and strong, reminding me of my power, my purpose. The green floods my chest, opening my heart wide with love, compassion, and peace.

The blue clears my throat, freeing my voice, letting me speak my truth. The indigo streams into my brow, sharpening my vision, awakening my inner knowing. The violet crowns me, pouring pure light through me, connecting me to everything.

I am glowing now – every chakra, every part of me, alive and balanced. I can feel the energy flowing smoothly, like rivers of light moving through my body.

It feels as though the rainbow has become part of me. I am not separate from it. I am the rainbow.

And in this moment... I feel whole. Completely whole. The heaviness is gone, the shadows released. I feel recharged, radiant, at peace.

For the first time... I know what it means to be free."

Ann's Journey – Returning Home

"The rainbow light is still around me, but I can feel it softening now, becoming part of me instead of surrounding me. It's settling deep into every cell, as though my body itself is glowing with all the colours of creation.

Ahead of me I see the doorway. It is open, waiting. I step forward, slowly, reverently, carrying the light with me. As I pass through, I look back once… and I know I can return here whenever I am called. The door closes gently behind me.

Now I see the stairs again. They look different – brighter, shining as though lit from within. Each step feels steady and strong beneath my feet. I descend slowly, calmly, carrying peace with me.

With every step, I feel myself returning to the present… to my own body… to this room.

One... my breath deepens. Two... warmth is returning to my hands and feet. Three... my body feels lighter, freer, alive. Four… I feel clarity in my mind, calm in my heart. Five… my eyes are opening.

Oh… everything looks different. The colours in the room are brighter. My body feels strong, clear, as though a great weight has been lifted.

I feel changed. My eyes… I can feel them shining. There is life in them, light in them. For the first time in years, I feel truly myself. Whole, free… and ready to live."*

Chapter 15: The Fourth Session – The Enchanted Spectacles

A week slipped by in what felt like a heartbeat, and soon Ann was back for her fourth session. She carried herself differently now – lighter, more at ease, as though a great burden had truly been lifted. Yet in her eyes there was also curiosity, an eagerness. She knew by now that each journey would take her somewhere unexpected, somewhere that held the power to transform her.

This time, I told her, she would be given the gift of *sight* – not ordinary sight, but the ability to perceive what lies hidden beneath the surface of life.

"Ann," I explained gently, "in this session you will be shown a pair of enchanted spectacles. They are no ordinary glasses. When you place them upon your face, the world will change. You will see beyond appearances, beyond illusions. You will see truth – the unseen threads, the hidden stories, the deeper meaning in all that surrounds you.

The spectacles will not frighten you. They will only reveal what you are ready to see. Perhaps the true nature of people in your life. Perhaps the hidden beauty in ordinary places. Perhaps even glimpses of lives or presences you could not see before. Whatever they show you, it will be for your healing and your growth.

When the time is right, you may take them off. But the vision they awaken within you will remain, long after the journey has ended."

Ann listened intently, her hands resting softly on her lap, her breath already deepening as though her spirit knew what was to come. She gave a small nod, ready to begin.

And so, I guided her once more into trance.

Ann's Journey – The Enchanted Spectacles

"I see them... oh, I see them. The spectacles. They're not like any glasses I've ever seen. They shimmer, as though they're made of crystal and light, yet they look ancient – older than time itself.

I can feel it... they were made before mankind, by hands – no, by beings – who understood truths that we have forgotten. The ancients created them, knowing that one day in history, humanity would need them again. They hid them, kept them safe, waiting for this moment.

They're here for me now.

I reached out... I'm almost afraid to touch them, they're so powerful, but they're warm in my hands, humming softly, alive.

I lift them to my face, and as soon as I put them on... oh... everything shifts.

The world is not what it seemed. The air ripples with colours, threads, lights moving between people, places, even the stones beneath my feet. I can see energy flowing, stories whispering in the shadows, truths that were hidden revealed in front of me.

And now... oh... I'm falling. Dropping through time. Faster and faster, as though the spectacles themselves are pulling me.

I land in another life. I can feel it – I'm not Ann anymore. My hands, my body, they're different. I'm living in another skin. The feelings that rise in me are not mine – fear, longing, sorrow – but they're so strong, they've been living in me all the same.

I understand now. The spectacles don't just show me what is hidden – they carry me back to relive the life where these feelings were first born.

I see now... this isn't only about healing myself. This is about healing the past. About returning what was never mine, and setting both of us free.

The spectacles are more than vision – they are a bridge through time."*

Ann's Journey – Through the Enchanted Spectacles

"I'm falling... falling still... and now I land. The ground is hard beneath my feet. Dust rises with every step. The air is dry, heavy with smoke and the smell of fire.

I look down at myself – my clothes are rough, simple, worn from work. My hands... they're calloused, strong, stained with dirt. They are not mine. I feel the weight of a man's body – broad, weary, burdened.

The year... I can hear people speaking, their voices carrying words and tones from another time. 1347. Oh... it's the time of the plague. The Black Death is sweeping through villages, towns, everything.

I see myself walking through narrow streets. The air is thick with fear. People look at one another with suspicion, as though every glance could carry death. Families are broken, children orphaned. The bells toll endlessly.

I feel the grief pressing in on me. Not just my own – the grief of the whole world. Despair that clings like smoke. Loneliness so sharp it cuts. The fear of losing everyone I love – my wife, my children. I feel it all inside me, heavy, choking.

And yet... deep down, I know these feelings do not belong to me, Ann. They are his. They were born in this time, in this body. He lived them, but somehow, across the centuries, I carried them too.

The spectacles show me the truth: the sadness, the fear, the hopelessness I have felt in my life are reflections. Echoes. They were never mine to bear.

My chest tightens... but with it comes understanding. I see now why I must be here. To honour him, to release what was his, and to set us both free."

Ann's Journey – The Release

"The weight in my chest is unbearable now... the grief, the fear, the loneliness. I can feel the cries of that time, the wailing in the streets, the silence of homes emptied too soon. It's pressing against my ribs, it feels as if I could break.

But I know... I know these feelings are not mine. They belong to him – the man whose eyes I now see through. His sorrow, his despair, his terror of losing his children, his wife, his world. He carried them. Not me.

My lips are trembling, but I force the words out, haltingly, as if they're tearing free from my very soul:

'I will honour your memory, but I cannot relive your life. The sadness, the fear, the unhappiness, the loneliness, the fear of losing my children... they are not mine. The insecurities are yours. All these feelings I have been holding onto... I will return them to you now.'

The air shifts. A darkness I hadn't realised was inside me begins to rise – a thick, heavy smoke uncoiling from my chest. It swirls, it gathers, and then it flows into him – into the man, my ancestor, my reflection.

And something astonishing happens. His back straightens. His eyes, once clouded with despair, filled with clarity. He looks at me – through me – and I can see gratitude shining there.

The grief is no longer bound to either of us. It's dissolving, breaking apart, carried away like ashes on the wind.

And in its place, something else flows forward. Strength. Resilience. Love. His spirit, unbroken, rises and fills me. His courage crosses the centuries and settles into my bones.

I gasp – my chest feels wide open, as though I can finally breathe after years of suffocation. A warmth spreads through me, golden, radiant.

And then... I feel it ripple. Backwards and forwards. Into the past, into the present. Into him. Into me. Into the countless lives tied by that thread. The release is not only mine – it's for all of us.

The sorrow has ended. The healing has begun.

For the first time, I feel whole. For the first time, he is free."

Ann's Journey – Cutting the Thread

"The release has lifted, but I can still see it... a thread. It stretches from him, in the year 1347, all the way into me here and now. It's thin, but strong – like a cord woven out of sorrow and fear. It's what tied me to his life, what carried his grief into mine.

I watch it pulse, dark and heavy. And I know… it must be cut.

In my hand, light gathers. A pure, bright beam, flowing from my palm like fire made of love. I raise it, trembling at first, but then steady, strong.

With a single sweep, I cut the thread.

The cord snaps silently – and at once, it unravels into sparks of golden dust, scattering into the air like stars.

As it dissolves, I feel the pull in my chest vanish. The weight is gone. The tie of suffering between past and present has been severed.

But I am not severed from him. The love, the strength, the dignity remain. Only the pain has been released.

The air shimmers around me. The web of threads that once tangled with sorrow is lighter now, glowing with colours of peace.

I whisper through tears: *'You are honoured. You are remembered. But you are free… and so am I.'*

And for the first time, I feel the bridge between past and present shining only with love."

Ann's Journey – The Rainbow of Renewal

"The thread has dissolved into golden dust, and the space around me is glowing, shimmering with light. And now… oh… colours are rushing toward me. Not just one – all of them.

A rainbow. The most beautiful rainbow I have ever seen. It pours out of the air, out of the earth, out of the very fabric of time itself. It surrounds me, flows through me, and enters every part of me.

Red seeps into the base of my spine, warm and steady, rooting me deep into the earth. I feel strong, grounded, and unshakable. Orange ripples into my belly, alive and joyful, opening me to flow, to creation, to delight in life.

Yellow bursts into my centre, blazing like the sun, filling me with confidence, strength, and radiant power. Green floods my heart, gentle yet vast, washing away every trace of loneliness, filling me with love that overflows beyond myself.

Blue streams into my throat, cool and clear, releasing the words I never spoke, giving me my voice back, true and free.

Indigo blooms in my brow, rich and deep, showing me visions, wisdom, truths I had always carried but never trusted.

Violet crowns me, showering down from above, connecting me to all-that-is, to the divine, to the universe itself.

The colours swirl together now, blending, weaving into every cell of my being. I am not separate from them – I *am* them. I am a living rainbow, shining with light from root to crown.

Every fear, every sorrow, every burden I carried has been washed away. In its place, strength, joy, and love pulse through me like rivers of light.

I am recharged. I am whole. I am free.

And for the first time, I feel not only healed… I feel radiant. As though the universe itself is shining through me."

Ann's Journey – The Gift of Forgiveness

"The rainbow is still flowing through me, but now it gathers in my heart – green and gold, pulsing with love. And I know… it is time for forgiveness.

I close my eyes within this vision, and I see him – the ancestor, the man of 1347, who carried the grief and fear that flowed into me. He is standing before me once more, but now he is different. His face is clear, his shoulders lifted, his spirit lighter. He is free, yet he waits, as though there is one last thing to be spoken.

I whisper the words slowly, feeling them rise from the deepest part of me: *'I forgive you. Not because you were wrong, not because you meant harm, but because forgiveness sets us both free. I forgive you, because the cords have been cut. I forgive you, so that peace can live between us, not pain.'*

My voice trembles, but I keep speaking. *'When I look into your eyes, I feel love. And when you look into mine, I know… you feel the same. This is what remains. This is what endures.'*

Tears run down my cheeks, but they are not heavy tears. They are cleansing, light.

He smiles at me, and in that smile is everything – gratitude, pride, release. Around him, others gather. Ancestors I cannot name, faces I half-remember, presences I only sense. They are waving, reaching out to me, sending love that floods through my body like sunlight.

And then, a voice – soft, gentle, but unmistakable:

'It's time to live your life. We are proud of you. We are watching over you.'

The rainbow brightens, wrapping me in its embrace. I feel forgiven, and I feel forgiving. The past and present are at peace.

And in this moment, I know... love is all that remains."

Ann's Journey – The Return of Forgiveness

"The rainbow is softening now. The ancestors are still smiling, still waving, but they are fading into the light. Their words echo gently in me: *'Live your life. We are proud of you. We are watching over you.'*

I turn toward the door. It gleams white, brighter than before, a symbol of new beginnings. I step through, carrying their love with me. The door closes, but the love remains.

I see the stairs again, shining beneath my feet. I descend slowly, peacefully, each step grounding me back into my body, into this moment.

One... my breath deepens. Two... my fingers tingle, warm and alive. Three... my whole body feels lighter, as though the weight of lifetimes has been lifted. Four... a calmness spreads through me, steady, radiant. Five... I open my eyes."

The Guide's Reflection

As Ann's eyes fluttered open, I knew before she spoke that something extraordinary had happened. The room itself felt different, as though infused with the quiet hum of her forgiveness.

Her face was radiant, her cheeks glowing with colour. The lines of strain I had once seen there were gone, replaced by softness. Her eyes shone – not only clear, but luminous, as if reflecting the rainbow light she had just carried through her body.

She exhaled a long, steady breath, and a smile broke across her face. It wasn't forced or fleeting – it was the smile of someone who had made peace with something deep, ancient, and long unresolved.

"I forgave him," she whispered, her voice trembling with awe. "And in forgiving him… I forgave myself."

Her words hung in the air like a blessing. And I knew – forgiveness was not only her release, but her rebirth

Chapter 16: – The Book of Echoes

A week later, Ann returned once again. Already, she was lighter than the woman I had first met. Her eyes held calm, her shoulders were free, her laughter surfaced more easily. Yet she also carried a quiet anticipation – she knew by now that each journey revealed something deeper, and she was ready.

This time, I explained, she would be guided to a place where voices live on. A place where whispers of the forgotten still call to be heard.

"Ann," I said gently, "today you will be shown the *Book of Echoes*. It is no ordinary book. Its pages are not filled with stories written by hand, but with the living resonance of voices across time. Each page is a memory, an echo of those who were once silenced. When you open it, you will not only read their words – you will hear them. You may feel their sorrow, their joy, their longing. And through you, they will finally be remembered.

The echoes do not come to burden you, but to be released. By hearing them, by honouring them, you will help them find peace – and in doing so, you will uncover what they have left within you."

Ann's eyes closed, her breathing deepened, and I guided her once more into trance. She descended, found the door, and stepped through into the timeless space where the Book of Echoes awaited.

Ann's Voice – The Book of Echoes

"I see it now. A great book, larger than any I have ever seen. Its cover is dark, worn; almost alive with energy. It hums softly, as though waiting to be opened.

I touch it… and the surface is warm, pulsing like a heartbeat. Slowly, I open it.

Voices. They rise all at once, a thousand whispers, like wind rushing through trees. They're speaking in so many tongues, so many tones.

Some are crying, some are singing, some are silent but heavy with longing.

I turn a page, and one voice grows louder. A woman. She is weeping. She is saying, 'See me. Do not forget me.'

The sound pierces me. My chest tightens, tears fill my eyes. It is as if her sorrow has lived in me all along.

I whisper back: 'I hear you. I will not forget you.'

The weeping softens. Her voice fades, but not into silence – into peace.

I turn to another page. A child's laughter spills out, bright and clear. I smile without meaning to, my body lightening. The child says, 'Remember joy. It belongs to you.'

The echoes... they are not all grief. Some are reminders of love, of strength, of joy lost and found. Each voice that rises is a thread, a piece of the great tapestry I carry within me."

Ann's Journey – The Echo of a Forgotten Ancestor

"The pages are turning themselves now... slowly, carefully... until they stop.

A voice rises – soft at first, then stronger. A woman's voice. Her tone is strained, weary. She whispers, *'I was never heard... I was never seen.'*

I can feel it. Her sorrow, her invisibility. It hits me like a wave. My whole body aches as though I've carried her silence for years.

Images form on the page – she is working in a dim room, her hands raw from labour. Children cry around her, but no one helps. No one thanks her. She gives and gives, but she is unseen, forgotten even as she lives.

Tears sting my eyes. I feel her loneliness, her exhaustion, her despair of never being recognised. And suddenly, I know why I have so often felt unseen myself – it was never truly mine. It was hers. I have been carrying her echo.

My lips tremble, but I speak aloud to her: *'I see you. I hear you. I honour your life, your struggle, your love. But I cannot carry your silence any longer. I will return it to you now, with gratitude.'*

As the words leave me, I feel it – a weight lifting from my chest, as though the silence itself is draining out of me.

On the page, she lifts her head. For the first time, I saw her eyes. They are full of light, shining with relief. She whispers back: *'Thank you. Now I am free. And so are you.'*

Her image fades, but the warmth of her gratitude lingers in me. The ache I carried has been replaced by something else – a strength, a quiet dignity that is hers, gifted to me without the burden.

The page closes itself, and the echo softens, merging back into the great chorus of voices. But now, it is no longer weeping. It is singing."

Part 5

Chapter 17: An Invitation to You, the Reader

You have now walked beside Ann through her five journeys: into the vast embrace of the Universe, among the endless shelves of the Akashic Library, through the mysterious Enchanted Spectacles, and into the voices held within the Book of Echoes.

You have read of her tears, her release, her forgiveness, her return to wholeness. And perhaps, as you close these pages, a thought lingers in your mind: *This must be fiction. A fairy-tale. A beautiful story spun to comfort or to entertain.*

But let me ask you – what if you are wrong?

What if everything you have just read is not a story, but a doorway? What if the traumas you carry every day – the grief that weighs in your chest, the fears that haunt your sleep, the loneliness you cannot explain – are not yours at all?

What if you are, even now, reliving someone else's life?

A grandmother's unspoken sorrow. A grandfather's quiet despair. The silent echoes of wars, of losses, of broken hopes, still alive in your blood, in your breath, in the rhythm of your heart.

The suffering of humanity does not vanish when life ends. It travels forward. It lingers in the body, in the mind, in the spirit. Like threads stretched taut across centuries, it binds the past to the present. A bridge of time, unseen but unbroken, carrying both pain and love into those who come after.

Pause for a moment. Think of your own family. Have you ever noticed the resemblance between yourself and someone long gone – not in appearance, but in feeling?

A sadness that mirrors a grandmother's melancholy? A restlessness that echoes an uncle's unfulfilled dreams? A fear of loss that mirrors the grief of ancestors who buried children, who survived wars, who knew hunger and silence?

We already know that illness can pass through generations – cancer, diabetes, heart disease. But why do we not speak as easily of emotions being inherited too?

Of grief flowing through bloodlines? Of trauma whispering in dreams? Of fear etched into DNA as surely as colour into the eyes?

And now – imagine this.

Imagine being able to step back through time. To enter a life from long before your own. To meet the ancestor whose sorrow you have been unknowingly carrying. To give back their pain, with honour, with love, with reverence. To lay it down, once and for all – for them, and for yourself.

What would it feel like to breathe without their sorrow pressing on your chest?

What would it feel like to laugh, and know the laughter was entirely your own? What would it feel like to live – not weighed down by the burdens of the past, but illuminated by its wisdom, its strength, its love?

This is not fantasy. This is not fiction. This is real. I have seen it. I have guided it. I have witnessed the transformations with my own eyes.

So now I turn to you. Yes, you.

What if the heaviness you feel is not yours? What if the patterns you repeat are not your own? What if freedom is closer than you think?

Take a step back. Open your mind. Dare to imagine. Because when you do, the doorways appear. And when you walk through them, you do not walk alone.

The ancestors are waiting. The healing is waiting. Freedom is waiting.

And so the question is no longer, *Is it real?*

The question is: *Are you ready?*

The Bridge of Time

Now you are beginning to understand – to truly feel – that the suffering in this world is not separate, not isolated, not random. It is connected.

It stretches like a bridge across time, linking the past to the present, threading through bloodlines, through memories, through the quiet corners of the soul. It is a frequency, a vibration, an ancient current of energy that touches every one of us.

The tears you have cried may not have been yours alone. The fears that rise in you may have been born centuries ago. The loneliness, the grief, the ache – all of it, echoes. And yet, so too are the love, the hope, and the strength that flow through you.

We have discovered that it is possible to travel across this bridge – to move not in imagination, but in spirit, into the lives of those who came before. To see through their eyes, to feel their hearts beating within ours, to witness the moments that shaped them… and to set them free.

We can return to the places our ancestors once stood. We can meet those we thought were lost – the grandparents, the mothers, the fathers, the unspoken stories still waiting in the silence. And in doing so, we do not lose ourselves – we find ourselves.

For when we heal the past, we heal the present. And when we heal the present, we free the future.

So now I ask you...

What will your journey be? What doorway will open for you? What life is waiting to be remembered, to be seen, to be set free?

The stories you have read are not tales of fantasy – they are invitations. They are maps. They are real.

And they are calling you. Step forward. The next journey is waiting.

Part 6

Chapter 18: The Journey Beyond Time

What if the bridge of time runs both ways?

If we can walk backward to heal the wounds of the past, might we also step forward – into futures yet unborn?

Close your eyes and imagine. A time beyond our own, where the air itself hums with harmony. Where every disease has found its cure, every wound its balm, every soul its peace. A place where no one is forgotten, no one is left behind, and the knowledge of the ancients and the wisdom of the stars have finally come together.

Perhaps, even now, someone waits there – knowing you will arrive. Someone who recognises you across the ages, who has been expecting you. They will take your hand, guide you, and together you will help to heal not only the past, but the suffering of humanity that still exists in your present world.

This is not imagination; it is potential. For time is not a line, but a circle. The past and the future meet in the same light – the same love – that exists within you now.

So yes, it is possible.

Possible to step beyond the limits of your own timeline, to glimpse what may yet be, to bring back from that place the vibration of healing, hope, and renewal.

And when you do, you will not only touch the future, you will help to create it.

Where the Loveday Method Has Taken Me

You may still think this is fiction. What you have read – the journeys through time, the meetings with ancestors, the voices from the Akashic Library, the rainbow light of healing – are simply stories.

But this is where the Loveday Method has now taken me.

When I first began this work, I believed it was only about the past – about walking back through the threads of memory to heal the wounds carried through generations.

But then, something changed. The journeys began to stretch beyond what I understood. The doorway that once opened into history began to open into possibility. And now, when I work with clients, we do not only go back. We go forward – far into the future.

It is a place that feels both distant and familiar. A time when the world has remembered how to heal itself.

Where illness, both mental and physical, has been understood and transformed. Where disease has no place because love and wisdom have found balance within the human spirit. It is a world not ruled by fear, but guided by understanding. Not by medicine alone, but by the harmony between science and spirit.

You may say, *"That cannot be true."* And perhaps you are right – perhaps it is beyond what we can yet prove. But I have seen it. I have felt it. I have walked with those who have travelled there in spirit and returned changed – their faces lighter, their hearts open, their eyes shining with something words cannot describe.

To be honest, I do not know exactly how it happens. But what I do know is this: anything is possible. When the heart opens, when the mind surrenders, when the soul remembers what it truly is – the impossible becomes reality.

The journeys I take people on now are unlike anything I could have imagined. They are vast and tender, filled with visions of light and cities that pulse with music instead of noise, where people live not in competition, but in cooperation. In this future, there is no hunger, no hatred, no separation.

Humanity has remembered its unity – that all pain, all joy, all healing, are shared. The people there welcome us as travellers returning home. They look into our eyes and say, *"We have been waiting for you. You carry the memory of what we have forgotten."*

You may think this sounds like a dream – a story, a hope, a fantasy. But tell me, what if it isn't? What if the future already exists, waiting for us to step into it? What if those who live there – healed, whole, and wise – are calling to us across time, urging us to remember who we are?

Because look at the world around you now. We are searching endlessly for answers. We chase medicine, we chase miracles, yet so often we forget the miracle that already lives within us.

We medicate the symptom, but we rarely heal the cause. We silence the pain, but we rarely listen to what it is trying to say. And the more we look outward, the more we lose the stillness that speaks within.

Perhaps it is time to look differently. To believe differently. To understand that healing is not found in a bottle, but in remembrance.

Remembrance of who we are. Of what we carry. Of the light that lives inside every cell, waiting to be awakened.

You see, the Loveday Method was never truly about hypnosis, or memory, or even regression. It is about awakening – awakening to the truth that time is not a line, but a circle; that we are the sum of all who came before, and the seed of all who will come after.

Through these journeys, people rediscover that the human spirit is vast – that it can move through centuries, cross dimensions, and speak with those who have loved us into being.

I am not a prophet. I am not a saint. I am simply a traveller, a guide, a pioneer searching for understanding in a world that has forgotten how to listen. But every time I witness a person heal – truly heal – I know that what we are touching is real.

Because the moment someone lets go of pain that was never theirs, they become radiant. When they forgive, they shine. When they remember, they become whole. And when they become whole, something shifts – not just in them, but in the world around them.

You can feel it, can't you? That quiet knowing deep inside you as you read these words – that what I'm saying touches something you already know, something ancient and true.

You are part of this story. You have always been.

The ancestors whisper behind you. The future calls ahead. And somewhere in between, in this breath, in this moment, you are standing on the bridge of time.

The question is not whether this is real. The question is whether you are ready to remember.

Because once you remember, there is no going back. Only forward – into light, into peace, into the extraordinary possibility of being fully, beautifully human again.

Part 7

Chapter 19: Ann's Journey – The World Beyond Time

"It begins as light. Not a beam, not a flash, but a living presence – breathing, pulsing, expanding. It draws me in, until I am no longer sure whether I am moving through it, or it through me. Then everything shifts.

The air feels different here. Thicker, sweeter, as though filled with unseen life. I'm standing, but the ground beneath my feet seems to rise and fall gently, like the rhythm of breath. The light around me is golden, but it isn't sunlight. It's a soft radiance that seems to come from everything – from the air, the trees, the stones, even from me.

And then I realise – I have stepped into the future.

I see a city in the distance, but it's nothing like the world I left behind. The shapes are organic, fluid – not built, but grown. Buildings of crystal and living vines spiral upward like trees reaching toward heaven. Rivers of light weave through the streets, flowing where water once ran. The air hums softly, like a thousand chimes carried on the wind.

People move gracefully through this place. They walk with purpose, but not with hurry. There is no sense of rush, no anxiety. Each step is deliberate, peaceful, connected. Their faces are radiant, their eyes alive with calm intelligence and warmth.

When they see me, they stop – not in surprise, but in welcome. One by one, they smile. Their smiles hold recognition, as though they already know me. A tall woman with silver hair and skin that seems to glow faintly steps forward. Her eyes are the colour of the dawn.

'Welcome,' she says. 'We have been waiting for you.'

Her voice is like music – not spoken sound, but vibration. It travels through me, resonating in my chest, aligning something deep within.

'You come from the age of forgetting,' she continues. 'We are in the age of remembering.'

She gestures for me to follow, and we walk together through wide gardens that pulse with colour. The flowers open as we pass, releasing light instead of fragrance. I reach out to touch one – its petals feel like silk woven from air, dissolving softly against my skin.

Everywhere I look, there is harmony. People are gathered in small circles under trees, their hands joined, eyes closed, energy flowing between them in gentle spirals of colour. Some sit beside pools of shimmering liquid light. Others stand with their palms raised toward the sky, absorbing sunlight that seems to carry nourishment directly into their bodies.

'There is no sickness here,' the woman says. 'There is no need for what you once called medicine. Healing has returned to its original form – understanding.'

She places her hand over her heart, then over mine. 'We learned that disease is not punishment. It is communication – the body's way of asking for balance. Once we listened, once we remembered how to love without condition, the imbalance ended. The body remembered how to heal itself.'

I feel her touch ripple through me. It's as if a thousand tiny lights awaken inside my chest, my cells singing softly. The tension I didn't know I was holding releases in waves.

She leads me into a great hall, open to the sky. In the centre, there is a sphere of light suspended in mid-air, rotating slowly. Within it, I can see galaxies, colours, movements of pure energy.

'This,' she says, 'is the Memory of Humanity – a living record of every life, every choice, and every moment. From it, we learn not by study, but by resonance. The past is not forgotten. It is healed. The future is not feared. It is guided.'

I step closer. As I gaze into the sphere, I see faces – countless faces, including my own, and the ones I love. They are all connected, each life shining like a thread in a vast web of light.

Tears fill my eyes. I whisper, 'We are all one.'

The woman nods. 'You always were. You just forgot.'

Her words break something open inside me. I feel warmth flood through my body – gentle, radiant, unstoppable. It moves from my heart outward, into every cell, every thought, every memory. I can feel the ancient wounds of my lineage dissolving, layer by layer. The grief that once belonged to ancestors, the fear, the loss – all melting away in this light.

For the first time, I understand: healing is not about changing what was, but about remembering what has always been whole.

The woman looks at me again, smiling. 'Take this knowledge back with you. Bring it to your time. Tell them that the future already exists – within them. Tell them that love is the cure they have been seeking.'

The city begins to fade. The people's faces remain for a moment longer – serene, luminous, and eternal. Then they, too, become light.

I am rising now, lifted gently as though by invisible hands. The light folds around me, wrapping me in warmth, carrying me home. I hear the woman's voice one last time:

'Do not doubt what you have seen. The future depends on remembering.'

The brilliance softens, and slowly I feel myself returning – the weight of my body, the rhythm of breath. But something fundamental has changed. The peace I felt there is still inside me, moving, expanding, alive.

I open my eyes, and the room is filled with light. For a moment, I wonder if it followed me back."

The Guide's Reflection

When Ann emerged, she sat in stillness for a long time. Her eyes glistened, her skin seemed to glow from within.

It wasn't imagination – there was something tangible in the air, as though the very atmosphere remembered the light she had touched.

When she finally spoke, her voice was soft, certain. "They've already found the cure," she said. "Not in science, not in medicine, but in remembering love. Everything else followed from that."

The words carried a power beyond explanation. It was as though truth itself had been spoken through her.

I watched her breathe, watched the light pulse gently through her. She wasn't the same woman who had walked in weeks ago – fearful, uncertain, weighed down by unseen burdens. This was a different Ann – grounded, open, and radiant.

I realised, in that moment, that she had become what she saw: a messenger between times.

And perhaps that is what we all are – messengers carrying fragments of the future back into the present, teaching the world that the cure for suffering has always been waiting within us.

The Truth Behind the Journeys

These images you have seen throughout this book are not fantasy – they are truth unveiled. They are windows into worlds my clients have entered, worlds that live just beyond the edge of what most call reality.

When I guide them into these journeys, something extraordinary happens. They do not *imagine* these lives – they *become* them.

They feel the pulse of another heartbeat inside their chest. They know the weight of another lifetime's sorrow, the ache of loss that once belonged to someone long gone; the trembling joy of reunion across centuries.

They feel it all – the sadness, the loneliness, the love, the hope – as if it were happening here and now, because in that sacred space, time itself dissolves.

You may tell yourself this is memory, imagination, suggestion – but you would be wrong. I have watched the change happen with my own eyes.

I have seen faces soften as lifetimes of pain melt away. I have seen tears fall from eyes that are no longer burdened by grief centuries old.

I have felt the stillness when peace finally returns – not just to one person, but to the entire lineage that flows through them.

This is not a story of make-believe. This is the remembering of humanity – a bridge between worlds, between souls, between who we were and who we are meant to be.

Every journey you have read is real. Every emotion, every colour, every vision is the truth of the soul speaking at last – saying, *I have lived, I have suffered, I have loved... and now, I am free.*

And as you read these words, perhaps you too will begin to wonder; What if the life you are living now carries whispers of another time?

What if healing the past could set you free in the present?

What if this, right now, is your invitation to remember?

The Bridge Forward

The Loveday Method had taken us across centuries – through the lives of ancestors, through the web of memory, through forgiveness and light. But this... this was something new.

It was no longer just healing the past. It was remembering the future.

The world Ann saw is not fantasy. It is potential – the reflection of what humanity can become when it remembers itself.

That future is already calling to us, waiting to be born through every act of love, every moment of courage, every person willing to believe that peace and healing are not distant dreams but living realities.

And now it waits for *you*.

Because the truth is simple and eternal. You are part of this bridge – between what was, what is, and what can be.

The light that healed Ann lives within you too. It has always been there.

All you need to do is remember.

Part 8

Chapter 20: Epilogue – The Awakening

The journeys are over, yet nothing truly ends. Ann has returned from her travels through the past and into the shimmering future, but her story lingers – like perfume in the air long after the flower has gone.

If you listen carefully, you can still hear it: a soft hum beneath the noise of the world, the sound of remembering.

For centuries, we have lived as though time were a straight road and we its weary travellers, always moving forward, always leaving behind.

But what if time is not a road at all? What if it is a great circle, alive and breathing, and we are the light that moves through it – each spark igniting the next, each life touching another?

Every thought you think, every emotion you release, ripples across that circle. Every kindness, every act of forgiveness, every breath of compassion travels outward and returns, carrying with it the power to heal. We are not separate from the past or the future; we are the bridge between them. Each of us is both ancestor and descendant, both question and answer.

Perhaps this is what the Loveday Method has always been trying to show: that healing is not about fixing something broken, but about remembering what was never lost. When we remember, we reconnect the circle. When we forgive, the echoes quieten. When we love, the whole of time leans closer.

Look again at the world around you. Every person you pass on the street carries a story older than themselves – threads of laughter, grief, endurance. Every child born today inherits not just DNA but the dreams of those who came before. Even the earth beneath your feet remembers: every raindrop once a tear, every breeze once a whisper from another life.

We have been taught to believe only in what we can touch.

But there is more. There is always more. Close your eyes for a moment and feel the pulse in your chest. That rhythm is not only your own; it is the heartbeat of generations.

It is your grandmother's lullaby, your great-grandfather's prayer, the first cry of the first human who ever dared to love. All of it lives within you.

This is why healing is possible. Because life itself is remembering. Because the love that created the universe has never stopped creating.

So imagine, if you will, a world that has learned this truth. A world where no one is afraid of their own reflection, because they know they are looking at the past and the future at once.

A world where medicine and spirit walk hand in hand; where scientists listen to dreams, and healers honour science; where compassion is not a weakness but a force.

A world in which every disease, physical or emotional, is understood as a message calling us back to balance – and every act of love answers that call.

You have glimpsed that world through Ann's eyes. Now you are part of it, because simply reading, simply imagining, begins to build it.

The future is not waiting somewhere ahead; it is forming now. With every choice you make. With every moment you choose understanding over judgment. With every breath that remembers to be kind.

When you close this book, do not think of it as an ending. Think of it as the opening of a door. Behind that door, the ancestors wait, smiling. Beyond it, the future glows, already healed, already whole, waiting for you to walk toward it.

You are not alone. You have never been alone. The light that guided Ann through her journeys burns quietly in you, too. It has always been there – patient, eternal, ready.

Listen.

There it is: the low hum of the universe turning, the sound of time remembering itself through your heartbeat.

Take one deep breath. Let it fill you. Let it remind you that everything you've read – every echo, every colour, every thread of light – is a map of what the human spirit can become when it dares to believe in its own magnificence.

The story continues now, in your hands, in your life, in the invisible bridge that connects all living things.

Walk across it. Carry the light. Become the healing.

Author's Note – A Message from the Heart

As you reach the end of this book, I want to thank you – not just for reading, but for feeling. Every page you have turned has been part of a shared journey: mine, Ann's, and perhaps, in some quiet way, yours too.

When I first began writing, I never imagined where these stories would lead. What started as curiosity became revelation; what began as healing for others became healing for myself. The Loveday Method was not something I *invented* – it was something I *remembered*.

Through the years, I have watched people rediscover parts of themselves they thought lost forever. I have seen tears fall and pain dissolve, replaced by lightness, laughter, and peace. I have witnessed people step through their own doors, meet ancestors long gone, and find forgiveness that rippled across lifetimes. And yes – I have seen glimpses of the future, too: radiant, healed, whole.

I do not claim to have all the answers. I am still learning, still listening, still walking the bridge between worlds.
But what I know with absolute certainty is that love is real.
Love transcends time, body, distance, and death. It is the thread that connects every life to every other, the language the universe never stops speaking.

The Loveday Method is not just a process – it is a remembrance. A way of returning to that inner knowing that whispers: *you are more than a name, more than a story, more than a single lifetime.* It is about stepping beyond the noise of the world to hear the quiet voice that says, *you are light, and you are loved, and you are never alone.*

If you have felt something stir inside you as you read – a warmth, a longing, a sudden peace – that is where your journey begins. Do not rush it. Simply allow it. Open yourself to the possibility that the unseen world is speaking to you, gently, patiently, with love.

Every time you forgive, you heal the past. Every time you love, you create the future. And every time you breathe with gratitude, you align yourself with the rhythm of the universe itself.

Whether you call it memory, soul, spirit, or energy – it does not matter. What matters is that you remember: you are part of something vast, ancient, and beautiful. You belong to a story that began long before your first breath and will continue long after your last.

So as you close this book, take a moment of stillness. Feel your own heartbeat. That is the drum of life, the echo of every ancestor who ever lived and every descendant yet to be born. Let it remind you that nothing is separate. That love, in its purest form, is eternal.

Thank you for walking this path with me – for daring to question, for allowing yourself to wonder, for opening your heart to the impossible.

If these stories have touched you, if they have opened something within you, then they have already done their work. Carry what you have found here into your world – into your relationships, your healing, your hope.

The journey continues, always. And perhaps, one day, when you are ready, we shall meet again, somewhere between the past and the future, somewhere upon the bridge of time.

Until then, walk gently, love deeply, and never forget, you are the light you've been searching for.

Dedication

To all who came before, whose lives and loves still move within us, and to all who are yet to come, may your path be lighter because we remembered.

To every soul searching for peace, every heart still learning to forgive, and every spirit brave enough to believe there is more. This book is for you.

May it guide you home to yourself.

Chapter 21: A Sign from the Universe

I wasn't sure whether to tell this story. Some things lose their magic when they're explained too quickly, and what happened to Ann deserves to breathe in silence for a moment. But I want you to know her name, because she has a beautiful heart and her courage has carried light into many other lives.

When Ann first began her sessions she was fragile, worn by too many months of trying to be strong. There was a weight in her eyes that spoke of a long struggle: illness, uncertainty, loneliness. Yet even in that fragility there was a spark – something quiet but unyielding that said, *I am still here.*

Each time she entered the deep state, the veil between her world and the other grew thinner. She began to trust the stillness, to listen to what it wanted to show her.

And on this particular day, near the end of her journey, I felt the air change again. She had reached the door, the symbolic doorway that marks the passage back into waking life.

Her breathing was calm, her energy soft. I said to her, as I often did at the close of a session, "Before you return, look around. There may be a gift waiting for you – a message that everything will be all right."

There was a long pause. Then she whispered, "I see two rag dolls."

Her voice trembled, uncertain. "Do you know what they mean?" I asked.

She shook her head. "No... not yet."

"Then trust that you will," I told her. "Sometimes the meaning travels slower than the message."

She took a deep breath, turned toward the shining stairs, and descended gently back through the layers of light until her body was here again.

When she opened her eyes there was peace in them, but also curiosity. "I wonder," she said softly, "what those dolls were trying to tell me."

We left it there.

Two days later my phone vibrated. It was a message from Ann:

"You won't believe this. I went back to work today after all those months away. It was emotional – I was nervous, but happy.

I work in the charity shop, and when I sat down at the counter, there on the desk were two rag dolls. Exactly like the ones I saw. How is that possible?"

She sent a picture with the message. Two worn dolls, sitting side by side, their faces smiling as though they had been waiting for her.

I stared at the photo for a long time. It would be easy to call it coincidence. But there was something about it – something quiet and deliberate – that felt like the universe exhaling a secret.

Perhaps the dolls were simply a sign that Ann was not alone, a small proof that the unseen world listens and answers in its own gentle ways.

Perhaps, in the moment she saw them, her future and her present had briefly touched, reminding her that healing doesn't end when the eyes open; it continues in the small miracles of ordinary life.

When we spoke later, Ann said the dolls made her feel safe. "They were smiling at me," she said. "I felt as if someone was telling me, You've done it. You can go back into the world now."

And maybe that was the message all along.

Maybe they were never about prediction or magic, but reassurance – an echo of love made visible for one brief, perfect moment.

I still have that photograph saved. Whenever I doubt, I look at it and remember: the world is kinder and more mysterious than we allow ourselves to believe. Sometimes, all it takes to see it is the courage of someone like Ann – and two little rag dolls sitting patiently on a counter, waiting to remind us that everything, somehow, will be all right.

Reflection – What the Dolls Taught Me

When I think of Ann's dolls, I no longer ask *how* they appeared. I ask *why*.

In the work I do, signs often arrive disguised as simple things: a feather on a doorstep, a song at the right moment, two small dolls on a counter. They are not proof; they are permission – tiny doorways reminding us that the visible and the invisible are never very far apart.

For me, the dolls came to symbolise return. Two figures, side by side, sewn from scraps yet whole. They seemed to say that the parts of ourselves we think are lost can always be stitched back together, that love is the thread that never breaks.

For Ann, they meant safety: a reassurance that she could step back into the world and be held by it again. For me, they were a quiet lesson in trust. The Loveday Method is not about controlling the unknown; it is about opening to it, allowing mystery to meet us in its own way.

We can spend a lifetime trying to explain miracles, or we can simply recognise them when they appear. Two rag dolls in a charity shop taught me that. They reminded me that healing is not always thunder and revelation.

Sometimes it is as soft as cloth, as humble as thread, as steady as a smile waiting on a desk to say, *You are safe. You are home.*

The Threads Continue

After Ann's session and the sign of the two dolls, I found myself thinking often about how her story might unfold from here.

Would she see more signs? Would her life begin to weave itself into new patterns, free from the echoes of the past? The truth is, I didn't need to know. Healing, once awakened, has its own quiet rhythm – it continues to move long after the session ends.

Each time someone journeys through the Loveday Method, I am reminded that we are all part of the same tapestry. Every release sends a vibration outward; every act of forgiveness lights another corner of the web. One person's awakening ripples through families, through generations, through time itself.

Ann's story is not finished. Nor is mine. Nor is yours. Because the work does not belong to one person – it belongs to the collective soul of humanity, still remembering itself after centuries of forgetting.

What began as a single woman's search for healing has become a mirror, reflecting something larger: the truth that each of us is connected by invisible threads of memory and love.

These threads do not bind us; they guide us. They lead us to understanding, to compassion, to the realisation that every life we touch is, in some way, our own.

And so the journey continues – from past to present, and now into what lies ahead. For beyond the echoes and the signs, beyond the lives remembered and the pain released, there is still another story waiting to be told.

A story about what happens when we begin to live fully in the light of everything we have remembered.

That is where we go next. That is where the bridge leads.

Part 9

Chapter 22: The Bridge Between Worlds – A New Beginning

Every story must find its turning point – that moment when the path widens, and what once belonged to one soul becomes the song of many. Ann's journey was such a moment.

Through her courage, something opened – not only for her, but for all who would come after. Each time she stepped through a door, she left it slightly ajar, allowing light to spill into the world for others to follow.

And I began to understand that the Loveday Method was never meant to be confined to one person's healing. It was always a bridge. A bridge between lives, between generations, between worlds.

We are all walking that bridge, though few of us realise it. We walk it when we dream of those we've lost. We walk it when we feel emotions we cannot explain.

We walk it when a place, a song, or a scent moves us so deeply that time itself seems to pause. In those moments, the past is not gone – it is touching us, reminding us that nothing real can ever be lost.

When you begin to see life in this way, everything changes. Grief softens. Fear loosens. The heart begins to recognise that what we call death is merely a doorway, and what we call the end is often the beginning of something vast and luminous.

The Loveday Method taught me this again and again; that love is not bound by time, and memory is not limited to the mind. Our ancestors live not only in our blood, but in our gestures, our dreams, our sudden tears and unexplainable joys.

They are the unseen companions who walk beside us, whispering guidance through intuition and chance. When we heal, we heal for them too. When we forgive, they are released. When we love, the circle closes – whole, unbroken, eternal.

I often wonder if this is what humanity is moving toward – a remembering, a reunion. Perhaps one day we will no longer need doors or visions to reach the other side.

Perhaps the veil will thin so gently that we will live fully in both worlds at once: the visible and the invisible, the past and the future, united in the present.

That, to me, is the new beginning. Not a world divided by belief and disbelief, science and spirit, body and soul – but a world where everything works together in harmony.

Where understanding replaces fear, and compassion becomes our first language. Where healing is no longer an exception, but a way of life.

You are part of that new beginning. Every time you read these words with an open heart, you are crossing the bridge. Every time you remember a loved one and feel peace instead of pain, you are helping to weave the worlds closer together. Every time you choose love over fear, you build another plank in that shining bridge between time and eternity.

And as we walk together, the bridge strengthens. The threads of light grow brighter. The universe itself seems to lean forward, watching, waiting, whispering, *Yes... they are remembering.*

So let this be your invitation: Step onto the bridge. Trust what you feel. The ancestors are waiting. The future is calling. And somewhere, between the two, the light of a new world is beginning to rise.

Final Words – Until the World Listens

So I keep writing.

I write for the ones who are searching, for those who feel the ache of something they cannot name. I write for the hearts that have forgotten their own light, for the souls that have grown tired of waiting for proof.

I write because I believe – not in fantasy, but in possibility. I believe that love remembers. That pain can be undone. That healing is not a miracle reserved for the few, but a birth right waiting for all.

Perhaps the world is not ready yet. Perhaps these words will lie quietly for years, like seeds buried deep in the dark earth, waiting for the right season to bloom.

But still, I write.

Because somewhere, in the near or distant future. Someone will open this book. They will turn the first page, and something inside them will stir, a faint whisper, a spark, a knowing.

They will feel it: the truth that has travelled through time to find them. And in that moment, the circle will complete itself. The bridge will shine a little brighter. Humanity will take another breath of remembrance.

I may not be here to see it. But I will feel it – in the great tapestry of time, in the pulse of the universe that carries every story, every echo, every soul.

So I keep writing. Not to convince, but to remind. Not to prove, but to awaken. Because one day, whether in this lifetime or another, the world will listen. And when it does, it will remember. It will remember that love never dies; that light never fades; and that healing, once begun, never ends.

Until that day, I will keep the pen moving, keep the flame burning, and keep the bridge open. For you. For me. For all of us, until the world is ready to believe.

Geoffrey E Loveday – The Loveday Method

The Dawn of Remembering

There will come a morning when the air itself feels new. People will open their eyes and, for a breathless moment, see the world as it truly is: not a battlefield of broken lives, but a web of light – each thread a pulse of kindness, each life a spark of the same fire.

The wars of the heart will have quietened. The noise of fear will have faded to a distant echo. In its place there will be a hum, low and steady, like the heartbeat of the earth. It will remind us that everything has always been connected: every river to every tear, every breath to every tree, every soul to every other.

In this dawn, the children will be born already knowing what we spent centuries trying to remember. They will speak to the animals, listen to the wind, and laugh at the old idea that one person could ever be separate from another.

The healers of this world will no longer fight disease; they will tend to harmony, guiding the body and the spirit to dance together again.

The scientists will study light, not as a thing to measure, but as a language to understand. The teachers will speak of compassion before arithmetic, of stillness before speech. And the earth, long patient, will sigh with relief as we learn once more to walk gently upon her skin.

This will not happen all at once. It will begin quietly – one person forgiving another, one heart opening, one act of kindness at a time. The world will change the way dawn comes: first a glimmer, then a glow, and then the sudden realisation that night has gone.

Perhaps that dawn is already rising. Perhaps, as you read these words, you can feel it stirring – the light of humanity waking from a long dream. If so, hold that feeling close.

It is the same light that Ann found in her journeys, the same light that travels through every story in these pages, the same light that waits within you.

When enough of us remember, the bridge between worlds will no longer be a dream. It will simply be life as it was always meant to be lived: whole, radiant, and awake.

And on that day, when humanity finally looks at itself and smiles with recognition, we will know that the miracle has already begun.

Closing Quote

"Time is not a line but a circle of light, and every soul is a spark that travels through it. When one spark remembers its brightness, the whole circle begins to shine."

– Loveday

About the Author

Geoffrey E. Loveday has spent much of his life listening – to people, to silence, and to the quiet language of the unseen.

His work began not as a profession but as a personal search for understanding – a way to make sense of the patterns of sorrow, love, and longing that seem to pass from one generation to the next.

Through years of experience, study, and deep reflection, that search grew into what is now known as **The Loveday Method** – a process that helps others explore the hidden landscapes of memory, emotion, and ancestry.

Guiding people through these journeys, Geoffrey has watched them rediscover forgotten parts of themselves, reconnect with their lineage, and release the inherited pain that has quietly shaped their lives.

He writes from a simple but profound belief: that healing is the natural movement of life itself; that every story, no matter how distant, longs to be heard and set free.

His books are part story, part meditation, and part invitation – written for anyone who has ever sensed that there is more to life than what meets the eye.

Today, Geoffrey continues his work of helping others to remember who they are – to walk the bridge between past and present, between the visible and the unseen.

His message is constant and clear: that love is the true bridge between all worlds, and that every act of compassion, every moment of forgiveness, brings humanity one step closer to wholeness.

For further information about the Loveday Method, upcoming writings, or future events, contact at:

www.liverpoolhypnosis.co.uk
www.mindlayers.com
thelovedaymethod.com
inheritedtherapy.com
Mobile: 07876028957

www.ingramcontent.com/pod-product-compliance
Lightning Source LLC
Chambersburg PA
CBHW070042040426
42333CB00041B/2017